Endorsements

"Michael is a profound seeker, teacher, and healer. This book invites the reader to lessen their burdens in life. It uses Michael's own life as an example and weaves together other individuals' stories. In addition, it provides a fantastic introduction and overview of many other authors and teachers. The book catalyzes your next step for personal healing and spiritual growth. It shows you how to live a connected life of service on your spiritual path." ~ Lee Murphy PhD, CEO Inspera Health

"How lucky for all of us on a spiritual path. The gifted Michael Lawrience has written a book to help us on our journey. His thoughtful guidance in this book is a must-have for all seekers." ~ Judy Rodgers, Co-founder The Peace Studio

"This book is filled with tools and techniques. It has many examples from people who have gone through healing processes with Michael. He is a gifted healer and author." ~ Carol Walker, Sound Transformational Practitioner

"Michael weaves wisdom with healing core wounds, brilliantly in his book. Years of his inner work shine through, to assist anyone who wants guidance to heal their wounds!

I highly recommend this book!" ~ Cynthia Barnard, Shaman Teacher/Healer

"Michael's book is a must for everyone on the path to raising consciousness. Reading his personal story is a positive confirmation. It is also a guidebook for healing the Inner Child."~ Teresa Peterson, Certified Bowenwork and Animal Bowen Practitioner

"Michael is a master energy healer, adding a new dimension to energy psychology. He weaves together personal experiences and practical dynamic tools for your healing. Healing the child within is at the heart of every therapeutic practice." ~ Maryanne, Licensed Marriage Family Therapist

"Michael combines his vast wisdom and gifts. He shares profound knowledge about self-evolution and healing in a digestible manner. This book is multi-tooled like a Swiss Army knife for your life journey." ~ Tricia Capello, Intuitive Artist

"This book offers a thorough guide in the path of healing and actualization. It explains how to examine your own inner processes. It's an invaluable guide to healing your life which is accessible to everyone." ~ Saari Soliz, Business Leader

"Michael's book is an amazing explanation of conscious and subconscious patterns. Patterns woven together with numerous insights from Self-Help gurus. Included are personal stories shedding Light on dysfunctional tendencies common to many of us.

"This book is designed for the seeker of transformation. It provides "how to" guidance to move past your limitations. A must read for everyone's Self-Help library." ~ M. Rende, Practitioner Myofascial Release

A Better Life Through Spiritual Growth and Higher Consciousness

Michael David Lawrience

A Better Life Through Spiritual Growth

and Higher Consciousness

Copyright © 2024 by Michael David Lawrience

All rights reserved. No part of this book may be used or reproduced by any means, graphic, electronic, or mechanical, including photocopying, recording, taping, or by any information storage retrieval system without the written permission of the publisher except in the case of brief quotations embodied in critical articles and reviews.

This book's information, ideas, and suggestions are not intended as a substitute for professional advice. Before following any suggestions contained in this book, consult your physician or mental health professional. Neither the author nor the publisher shall be liable or responsible for any loss or damage allegedly arising from your use or application of any information or suggestions in this book.

ISBN: 979-8-9868130-4-2

Library of Congress Control Number: 2024922643

Cover Design by: Vanimdesign.com

Sacred Life Publishers™

www.SacredLife.com

Printed in the United States of America

Contents

Endorsements i

Introduction xi

1 – Raising Consciousness:
    How to Deal with Life Challenges 1

2 – How to Better See and Begin Healing
    Your Childhood Trauma.. 11

3 – How to Heal Your Wounded Inner Child 25

4 – How to Better Reparent Your Inner Child 31

5 – Do You Know Your Wounded Inner Child Needs
    Healing?... 41

6 – Meditations to Better Heal Your Inner
    Child Trauma.. 51

7 – How to Heal Your Wounded,
    Suffering Inner Child 61

8 – Three Practical Steps for Healing Your Victim
    Inner Child 69

9 – Energy Healing to Heal Your Wounded
    Inner Child 77

10 – How Can Angels Best Help Healing
    Inner Child Trauma? 85

11 – Emotion Code: How to Best Heal Your Heart-Wall....93

12 – How to Overcome Drama Triangle of
     Relationship Victim, Rescuer, Abuser Conflict......103

13 – How to Overcome Drama Triangle of
     Relationship Victim Conflict........................113

14 – Subpersonalities: How to Better Recognize
     and Transform Them 121

15 – Codependency: How to Feel Your Best
     and Recover 133

16 – Five Core Symptoms of Codependency:
     How to Break Free 143

17 – Codependency: 12 Steps and Tips –
     How to Best Recover 155

18 – How to Best Deal with Stress and Overwhelm..........165

19 – Spiritual Growth: My Dark Night of the Soul.............179

20 – Embodying Divine Male and Female Archetypes for
     Better Health 187

21 – Self-Growth: How to Best Start Successful
     Shadow Work.......................................201

22 – How to Enjoy Defining Moments, Critical Choices
     and Pivotal People.................................211

23 – Benefits of Meditation:

    Unlocking Higher Consciousness............................ 235

24 – Spiritual Growth:

    How to Be in Higher Consciousness 249

25 – Service Consciousness:

    How to Live in the Present Moment 269

About the Author 281

Introduction

Welcome to a transformative exploration of inner truth and healing. As a seeker, spiritual teacher, and energy healer, I've discovered that every moment offers a lesson that can guide us on our journey. Through my own experiences and the narratives of others, I've come to realize the power of sharing our stories in fostering understanding and growth.

In these pages, you will find insights into healing childhood wounds, overcoming self-doubt, and nurturing self-esteem. Each chapter addresses vital themes such as healing the wounded inner child and recognizing the complexities of codependent relationships. Together, we will navigate the victim triangle and uncover the dysfunctional patterns that often hold us back.

This book is designed to support you in achieving inner spiritual growth and elevating your consciousness. May it inspire you to embrace your journey, fostering resilience and awakening a deeper understanding of yourself.

1 – Raising Consciousness: How to Deal with Your Life Challenges

> *Accept - then act. Whatever the present moment contains, accept it as if you had chosen it. Always work with it, not against it. Make it your friend and ally, not your enemy. This will miraculously transform your whole life.* ~ Eckhart Tolle, author of *The Power of Now*

This was one of the worst times of my life. When would I ever escape the hard work on the farm?

One day, an inspiration flashed in my sixteen-year-old teenage mind. Somehow, I would go to college. This decision transformed my life forever.

Overcoming Life Challenges

At the age of twenty-four, intuitively, I knew my most important goal, which involved emotional and spiritual growth. I have been on this journey of inner growth for seventy-seven years. I learned to face and overcome my life challenges, which has transformed my life.

Do you hate your life now? Do you feel like a prisoner without parole? What are your challenges? Finances, health, and or relationships?

Do Any of the Following Challenges Apply to You?

- Lack of love?
- Inner child controlling your life?
- Past childhood traumas keep resurfacing?
- Constant critical self-talk?
- Stress and overwhelm?
- Low self-esteem?
- Hating your life?
- Living in constant dissatisfaction?
- Wanting to be somewhere else?
- Wanting to do something different?
- No one to talk to about how to change your life?

Michael: *The challenges of my childhood trauma have affected my inner child. He wants recognition from others. The Jokester would crack off-hand jokes for attention. My child wanted people to tell him he was a great boy.*

For years, I created my pain and suffering. I resisted and fought my circumstances. Tiredness and fatigue exhausted me. I felt anger and closed down my emotions.

In my thirties, I looked and felt poker-faced, non-expressive, and numb. Numb represents the lowest level on the emotional scale.

Life challenges interfere with your quality of life or ability to achieve life goals. How do these physical, emotional, mental, or spiritual issues affect you?

Challenges have a habit of reappearing in different ways. They do this to get your attention. The longer you ignore them, the more difficult they become. So, as Tolle said, I started accepting *"Whatever the present moment contains."*

What I Learned

I learned how to stop resisting and surrender to the moment. This required many decades of continuous self-growth and perseverance.

I learned to go inside my body, feel the pain or tension, notice where it was, and breathe into it. Over time, the tension lessened. I also found a way to raise my consciousness.

Consciousness relates to your outer and inner awareness. You learn how to use higher awareness to achieve goals and improve your life.

Dealing with Challenges

- We attract that which we fear or fight. We strengthen that which we oppose/fight/resist.
- Do you want to create with fear or positive intent?
- Do you know you have a choice?
- What trauma hides behind the challenges?

Do you see trauma as negative? What if it is a challenge to overcome?

"Life isn't limited by what happens to you. It is how you react to what happens." ~ Gabor Mate, author of *When the Body Says No: The Cost of Hidden Stress*

In my book, *How to Deal with Your Life Challenges,* you explore childhood trauma, critical self-talk, self-esteem, and codependency are discussed. The book continues with stress, the dark night of the soul, and subconscious archetypes. Successful shadow work, critical choices, meditation, and spiritual growth are also included.

Explanation of Challenges to Begin Healing

- Heal childhood and family lineage trauma.
- Meditation to stop constant self-talk.
- Improve self-esteem.
- Recognize and begin to become less codependent.
- Practices for overwhelm and stress.
- Explanation of dark night of the soul.
- Male and female subconscious archetypes of power.
- Inner shadow work. (We all have shadows and gifts.)
- Defining moments, critical choices, and pivotal people.
- Divine energy and intuition.
- How to be in higher consciousness and awareness.

I wrote this book as a legacy of my inner emotional and spiritual journey of self-growth. This is my journey from age twenty-four to seventy-seven. My passion and gifts come alive in energy, healing, and teaching.

Michael: *I suffered and persevered through my challenges. For years, I questioned when I would ever discover my life purpose.*

Much of the time, I knocked my head against a perceived rock wall. I resisted and struggled rather than knowing how to surrender to the moment.

Unknowing to me, the challenge of every moment had a teaching. When I got the lesson, I moved forward.

Some of my experience consists of teaching troubled teens at group homes for eleven years. I taught self-esteem and recovery from codependency weekly to teens for eight years.

In phone consultations, my wife, Lyn, and I teach people how to heal trauma and transform consciousness.

I also studied JJ Hurtak's Keys of Enoch, *spiritual teachings on seven levels, for over thirty years. The* Keys of Enoch *prepare humankind for the quantum leap forward in communication with the worlds of Higher Evolutionary Intelligence.*

Conclusion: Life Challenges

- Do you accept your life challenges?
- Do you choose to keep moving forward?
- Do you savor/enjoy your life journey?

Beyond our personality awareness, we live in higher conscious awareness. In some, this is a dormant seed. In others, it has begun sprouting.

Start to face your challenges. Learn and practice the tools in this book daily. Your life will transform.

Start looking at your inner patterns of childhood wounding. Say "Yes" to notice and acknowledge pain in your body. Feel the discomfort and breathe into it. Your finances, health, and relationships may be affected. For further insights, I present the stories of two people's challenges. I know these people. They have explored spiritual growth and higher awareness for many years.

Each paths differs. You learn from your experiences and from being in relationships with others.

Alyson and Pat have been on an inner journey for most of their lives. They share their life challenges.

Alyson has been on a journey of inner growth for fifty years. She answers some questions about her life challenges.

Alyson: *I began my spiritual journey at age twenty-four. I read Carl Rogers book* On Becoming a Person *and went into therapy. Coming alive to consciousness and spiritual growth came at twenty-seven. I went through therapy with Stephen Wolinsky. Wolinsky is the author of dozens of books on consciousness. I experienced Reichian and Gestalt therapy in Wolinsky's groups. This led to Siddha Yoga Meditation. I followed this path for twenty-five years. The path is about seeing God in yourself and others.*

What would you have liked to know?

Alyson: *At age fifty, I was introduced to New Age teachings. It was a community of lightworkers, healers, and channelers. I had no idea how to discern false teachers from true teachers. As a result, I encountered good as well as traumatic experiences. I didn't know how to protect myself.*

What challenges did you have with your beliefs, health, and relationships?

Alyson: *I am grateful my spiritual path was always clearly laid out for me. Following my Higher Self resulted in a clear direction. My family, however, was affected both financially and emotionally. My husband provided support, although it impacted our relationship.*

My spiritual life has always been at the center of my mind. The path became painful when I greatly admired someone and wanted to be like them. Then, I discounted the Divine Being I AM. This occurred mainly in Arizona.

Alyson's Spiritual Path

She has studied *A Course in Miracles*. I like having Jesus/Holy Spirit as my guides. I also have Archangel Michael for protection and Archangel Raphael and MAP for healing.

Explanation of Modalities and Archangels

Reichian therapy looks at our attitudes. It also shows the ways we isolate because of trauma.

A Course in Miracles by Helen Schucman offers a practical approach to applying the teachings. It provides insights and exercises for personal growth and transformation.

Multitudes of Archangels exist. The most common include Michael, Gabriel, Raphael, Uriel, Metatron, and Sandalphon.

MAP—The MAP Healing Program is a process of healing the relationship between consciousness and trauma. Trauma is gently accessed and healed. You can contact a MAP Practitioner.

Pat has been on a journey of inner growth for many years. She answers some questions about her life challenges.

Pat: *I began my journey of self-growth at age thirty-four. At thirty-six, a more conscious growth began.*

What Problems Did You Have at the Beginning?

Pat: *I was crushed by the mystery of physical pain/ailments and inflammation. A feeling of deep depression descended upon me. Little community support isolated me. Certain family members drained and triggered my physical, mental, and emotional bodies.*

What Challenges Did You Have with Your Beliefs, Meditation, and Shifting Your Consciousness?

Pat: *Staying disciplined, struggling using tools I know work, continues. In addition, it took a while to build an internal recognition system. Then, I deciphered what I truly experienced. I questioned if the experience was even mine.*

I still slip into separating outside beliefs from my Divine identity. The removal of many layers has been slow and ongoing. Lastly, I take on other people's energies. I struggle with trust, for I doubt myself.

What Would You Have Liked to Know?

Pat: *In the beginning, everything is so new and confusing. I felt isolated. It was difficult to explain what I experienced. In addition, I trusted some people who were energy vampires.*

Energy vampires intentionally drain your emotional energy. These humans feed on your willingness to listen and care for them. They leave you exhausted and overwhelmed. This may be your spouse, your best friend, or your neighbor. Learn to set personal boundaries.

Pat: *Staying centered and calm, I developed discernment. I learned how to clear my energy.*

Start looking at your inner patterns of childhood wounding. Say "Yes" to notice and acknowledge pain in your body. Feel the discomfort and breathe into it. Your finances, health, and relationships may be affected.

2 – How to Better See and Begin Healing Your Childhood Trauma

Trauma is the invisible force that shapes our lives. It shapes the way we live, the way we love, and the way we make sense of the world. It is the root of our deepest wounds. ~ Gabor Mate, author of The Myth of Normal: Trauma, Illness and Healing in a Toxic Culture

The newly born child shrunk in fear. Its body, feeling unsafe and alone, wanted to go back to the womb. The child was me! I have felt unsafe all my life.

Did you experience trauma during your childhood?

Your childhood pain lies at the root of suffering. Also, later health challenges can result.

Childhood trauma may involve physical, sexual, and emotional abuse and neglect by parents.

Trauma includes some of the following:

1. Family dysfunction and separation.

2. Lack of emotional bonding between children and parents.
3. Poor parenting practices and witnessing violence between parents.

What kind of traumas were you exposed to?

How to Heal Childhood Trauma

Gabor Mate, M.D., as an expert on Addiction and Stress, shows how to heal childhood trauma.

"To heal addiction and stress, your inner child requires healing."

"Trauma is not what happened to you. Trauma is the wound that you sustained." ~ Gabor Mate, author of *The Myth of Normal*

Gabor Mate has six questions of self-inquiry for understanding your trauma.

1. What are you not saying "No" to in your life? (Family and Friends).
2. What do you miss out on due to your inability to assert yourself?
3. What body symptoms/pains do you overlook?
4. What is the hidden story behind your inability to say "No?"
5. Where did you learn that story? (Caregivers or parents.)
6. Where have you stopped yourself from saying "Yes?"

Answer these six questions for yourself. Write your answers in a notebook.

Here are some examples from my life.

1. What Are You Not Saying "No" to in Your Life?

A three-year-old child shakes. His father yells at him and he feels it best to keep quiet. The child learns to stifle crying.

He becomes the invisible one in the family. As a teen, he acts like a flower. Yet, his strongest desire is for others to see him.

I am that boy. I denied and suppressed emotions for a lot of my life.

My father, as an alcoholic addict, yelled and fought with my mother. I learned to stay quiet. Furthermore, I never talked to anyone in my family about my thoughts or feelings. A depressive pall covered the whole family of parents and five children. This cloud descended when my father sometimes wasn't fighting my mother. That occurred when he had no alcohol that day—a rare occasion.

Later, in relationships with women, I never felt safe expressing emotions. With my first girlfriend, in the first year, she used to drill me for hours. What did I feel? I had no idea. We both ended up emotionally drained on those days.

In my thirties, I dreaded saying no to girlfriends, including the one I lived with. I gave thousands of dollars for their cars or condos, and I paid the rent for the apartment we lived in. My inner child wanted kudos. As a result, my adult part allowed the inner child to control.

One day, I started seeing a hypnotist and learning self-hypnosis. After a few months, I had more courage and confidence. I told my girlfriend she had to move out on a certain day. She had stored all her boxes of belongings inside the entrance, towering to the ceiling for three years.

Fear of Saying No

I had a challenge saying No in my birth family. I had no idea how to stand up for myself. Instead, I went invisible. I said No to expressing my emotions. I said No to using my voice. I avoided confronting my father. I never told him to stop fighting with my mother. I dreaded saying No to girl friends' requests for a place to live. I never said No when they needed money.

2. What Do You Miss Out on Due to Your Inability to Assert Yourself?

I take care of everyone else's pain and problems. By taking care of everyone first, I neglect myself. I am the last to drink from the fountain for energy, so I am fatigued daily.

As a full-blown codependent for years, I took care of other's needs.

3. What Body Symptoms/Pains Do You Overlook?

"Emotional suppression is a silent stressor that can manifest as a physical disease." ~ Gabor Mate, author of *When the Body Says No*

I repressed emotions and felt chronic stress most of my life. It started as a young boy working on a farm in Alberta.

My father ignored me. Working on the farm, he seldom spoke to me. He kept all his thoughts and feelings private. As a teen, I yearned for him to teach me, for example, how farm machinery worked. Later, I searched for mentors in college professors.

As a teen, compulsive perfectionism dogged my every step. I stepped over cracks in the cement in a certain way for years.

I overlooked a congenital hernia and also a hernia developed over twenty years. Also, I over-stressed my adrenals and kidneys. I pushed hard against life to succeed. I constantly asked, "What was my life purpose?"

In my thirties, I began exploring my emotions and feeling in my body. In my seventies, I stopped resisting life, surrendered, and allowed Divine Grace to enter. Each time, consciousness shifted profoundly.

My journey of self-growth into greater levels of consciousness began at age twenty-four.

"Self-compassion and self-care are essential for maintaining a healthy body-mind connection." ~ Gabor Mate

The Following is a Client's Experience of Their Journey of Spiritual Growth.

Karen began her journey at the age of seventeen, exploring Christian religions. A lifelong search began in her early thirties.

Karen: *My interest involved healing and connection. I wanted more love in my life.*

In the beginning, Karen encountered many challenges.

- My family refused to accept my change. I dealt with judgments, disbelief, and doubt from them.
- I needed alone time to contemplate and meditate.
- No one to share with and ask questions. Later on, I attended events with like-minded people.
- I learned the power of Intention.
- Despite impatience, positive affirmations made a difference.
- I realized the same negativity resided within me when I judge others negatively.
- When I shared my insights, others had their viewpoints. They wanted to hang onto their version of "truth." I questioned my viewpoints.
- I had challenges with shifting my conscious awareness.
- It took practice to discover what I felt.
- I had to identify what I wanted.
- My consciousness constantly expanded. So, I attended healing workshops.
- Intention helped expansion.
- I tended to be more heart-centered rather than analytical. I discovered tools to deepen my Divine Connection.

What would have been helpful early on in my journey?

- I had a willingness to get into the trenches and work. There can be a slower rhythm for beginners.

- Surrounding myself with like-minded people.
- To have an example or mentor. How can I deepen my connection to the Divine, joy, love, and peace?

Karen ends, I am grateful for all the challenges that created who I AM now.

4. What is the Hidden Story Behind Your Inability to Say "No?"

I grew up on a cattle and grain farm. My father swam into alcoholism. He frequented the bar in our small town. At home, he drank rye whiskey down in the barn.

Our mother did all the work and raised five kids by herself. From her family upbringing, she became a workaholic.

I, as the eldest, unconsciously took over the father's role. This occurred at a young age. My father, being non-present, lived in his world. In my subconscious, I had to be strong. Also, I was responsible. I knew it was unsafe to express emotions. My father was an angry, brutal man. When drunk, he fought regularly with my mother.

I knew never to say "No" to my father. He would have beaten me. The daily farm work existed from dawn to dusk. Neither could I say "No" to my mother. I functioned as her reliable farm hand.

This is an example of being unable to say "No." One morning, with the rising sun, Mother and I walked out to one of the fields. Suddenly, I felt I couldn't do the heavy lifting of the stooks that day. (Stooks are bundles of cut grain that must be stacked together to dry.)

I was on the brink of breaking down and crying, but I damped down my feelings. We went to the field.

Over-Responsibility

I am more than responsible. Over-responsibility has always been part of my personality. My belief, "Only I can do it; It's all up to me."

Over-responsibility is a trauma response.

Do You Identify with Any Actions, Beliefs, or Feelings Below?

- Accept it's your fault your parents never loved you?
- Believe it's your "job" to take care of everyone?
- Feel separation within yourself – alone – different – unsafe?
- Felt less than, unloved, or unworthy?
- Doubted self?
- Give away your power?
- Inner child needs control?
- Lack of connection to the Divine?
- Rescuer – responsible for everyone's well-being?

I Identify With:

- I feel separation within myself – alone – different – unsafe.

- I doubted myself and felt less than, unloved, and unworthy.
- I believe it's my "job" to care for everyone.
- I am responsible for everyone's well-being – Rescuer.
- I give away my power.

I identified with the above for a good part of my life. Today, they affect me much less.

Trauma may manifest as people-pleasing and codependency in relationships.

5. Where Did You Learn That Story?

The following is a client's experience of their over-responsibility. My wife, Lyn, and I assisted in a phone session.

Pat describes her artistic practice. She meditates, tuning deeply into herself. Diving into her intuitive mind, she receives higher conscious awareness.

Pat: *In my session with Lyn and Michael, layers of past lives emerged. At that time, I made myself invisible. Part of me got trapped in the Shadow world. I had many lifetimes in this Shadow world. Fear and self-doubt existed. I also got caught up with Black Magic and greed. Lyn and Michael held the energy throughout the session. I pushed wealth away, as I had misused it previously. Being over-responsible, I blamed myself for taking on the Shadow energy, Mea Culpa.*

When you take on being over-responsible, a percentage is yours. You think it is all yours. A smaller percentage is yours, many times ten to thirty percent. The rest can be your father's or mother's family lineage. Another part can be the collective consciousness of humanity.

Pat: *At times, I misused my power. I was very hard on myself for the misuse. I surrendered, so now Lyn could invite Divine Grace to come in to assist. A lot of dark energy came out of my womb. I realized that as a young child, I had let my mother manipulate me. My mother had a challenge loving herself. My interest involved healing and connection. I wanted more love in my life.*

Michael: *I learned from the trauma of family dysfunction and separation. I learned my story from my father and mother. Both my father and mother experienced trauma growing up. My father never recovered. He gave up on life.*

6. Where Did You Learn That Story Continued?

Michael: *My mother handled her trauma the best way she knew. That meant making the best of life. She worked all the time, which resulted in making sure the family always had something to eat. She always wanted the best for everyone.*

I took on my father's trauma and anger subconsciously as my own. My subconscious belief involved healing him. I did this for most of my life. One day, I realized it was never my job.

With my mother, I learned to work hard and persevere regardless of challenges. These qualities exist also in my personality.

I learned my story from the trauma of a lack of emotional bonding with my father. I have to do everything myself. I am "less than." I never felt a bond with my father. He remained a stranger all my life.

An example: At age twenty, I lived in Hawaii for nine months. I enjoyed myself, matured, and made a lot of money. I came back to visit my parents on the farm for a few months before college. My uncle was also visiting. I excitedly told my father and uncle I wanted to share my experience of Hawaii. I did with my uncle. My father never sat with me. I believed he was jealous.

I learned my story of trauma from the poor parenting practices of my parents. When my father was young, he came over from Austria to Canada. He came with his mother. I gather he took care of his mother. Probably, he was very codependent, wanting to please her all the time.

My father had no experience parenting, and my mother also had little experience. My mother's mother died when she was young, so my mother took over cooking and cleaning on her father's farm. She took care of four brothers and her father into her late twenties.

Despite her challenges, my mother remained a loving being. Although we never talked about our feelings, I felt her love.

I learned my story of trauma from witnessing eighteen years of violence between my parents.

My father fought almost all the time with my mother. In his drunkenness, he would yell and demean my mother. We children put up with the rage in silence.

There were stories of fathers in farm families killing their families. It scared me as a teen.

One day, I was visiting, and the parents were fighting. My younger brother said, "I am going to shoot that 'so and so.'" My brother had a twenty-two rifle in his hands. Without thinking, I grabbed it from him. For many years, I wiped that memory out. I was terrified.

In my emotional repression, I never knew how to feel or express emotions.

7. Where Have You Stopped Yourself from Saying "Yes?"

A. Like me, do you struggle to say No?

I am a workaholic.

For most of my life, I have said yes to all obligations, both those others put on me and those I put on myself.

I stopped myself from saying Yes. Yes, to life, joy and relaxation.

B. What is the impact of you not saying No?

I am always serving others. I give my energy/life force away to everyone else first. As a result, I am fatigued most of the time. I am exhausted.

C. What is your hidden belief behind not saying No?

It is my job to look after everyone's needs first.

D. Who would I be if I learned to say a healthy No?

I would be in my power and sovereignty.

E. Where do I need to say a healthy Yes?

Say "Yes" to noticing and acknowledging pain in my body. Feel the discomfort and breathe into it. Stop working and take short breaks throughout the day. Do exercise, yoga, stretches, meditate, or go out briefly in nature. Say "Yes" to compassion for myself. Give loving attention to my body to relax and heal.

Spiritual growth connects you with your authentic Divine Self. My journey of self-growth into greater levels of consciousness began at age twenty-four. I have been on a path of Spiritual and Self-Growth for over fifty years.

Dealing with Life Challenges

1. How I Began Healing My Childhood Trauma in My Thirties

- Began feeling and expressing my emotions.
- I started using my voice.
- Began exploring my victim patterns, i.e., sinking into a pit of feeling sorry. I started exploring my codependency/people pleasing.
- I used the Six Steps of Focusing Method, opening up inner deeper feelings and intuition.

2. Feeling and surrender

- Continuing exploring emotions.
- Feeling my body more.
- Growing awareness of critical or positive thoughts.
- Becoming aware and choosing to stop resisting the moment.
- Surrendering and allowing Divine Grace/Love to enter.

Consciousness now shifts in a profound way. This has been a life journey.

3. Over-Responsibility: Over-Responsibility is a Trauma Response

- Noticing and changing beliefs – "It's all up to me."
- I am taking on other people's energy.
- I am asking: Out of 100%, how much is mine? It is, for example, 1 to 15% — the rest is the other person. I then deal only with mine.

4. Daily Saying a Healthy Yes

- Noticing and acknowledging pain in my body. Feeling the discomfort and breathing into it.
- Stop working and taking short breaks throughout the day.
- Doing short exercises, yoga, stretches, meditating, or going out briefly in nature.
- Allowing compassion for myself.
- Living loving attention to my body, relaxing, and healing.

3 – How to Heal Your Wounded Inner Child

The energy of mindfulness is the salve that will recognize and heal the child within. ~ Thich Nhat Hanh, Zen Master

Inner Child

My inner child ran my life. Unknown, he did this invisibly under the surface of my consciousness. He had control for almost half my life.

My inner child ran my life through drama and trauma.

I kept repeating the same stories in my mind of suffering.

My inner child carries the wounds from growing up with an emotionally distant father addicted to alcohol.

However, I am grateful beyond measure to my father. He gave me the freedom to explore my innocence and curiosity. In the groves of maple trees, I played fantasy cowboy games.

At ten, I played with my younger brother for hours during school breaks. We did this for two summers.

As a man, I never related to my inner child. I knew nothing about having an inner child. In addition, when I studied psychology at college, no one ever mentioned the inner child.

Yearning for a father, I considered two college professors father figures.

Inner Child Work

My inner child remained invisible and unknown to me until my early forties. My partner at the time told me she had a therapist who worked on healing her child. I began learning about my child. Desiring to know and express my emotions drove me. I also needed to learn about my needs in relationships.

I started reading John Bradshaw's *Reclaiming and Championing Your Inner Child.*

Today, I am aware of my inner child daily. As an adult, I disciple my child.

A few years later, I began teaching my hands-on energy healing system, which included healing the inner child. At this time, I realized the intensity of pain my wounded child had carried since childhood.

Over a decade later, my wife, Lyn, assisted me by refusing to accept being my emotional body. Your inner child connects to your emotions.

I numbed and avoided my emotions for two-thirds of my life. Therefore, instead of feeling and expressing my emotions, my wife did it for me. All my previous female partners had also done this in the past. I had been unaware of this as well, as they were.

One day, Lyn refused to do this. She explained that I needed to be responsible for my feelings. Therefore, I accepted and began to express my feelings a bit more.

I connect with my feelings easily now.

How many men like me unconsciously have their women carry their emotions for them?

The following is a client's experience of healing their childhood abuse. Your childhood wounds affect your adult self. My wife, Lyn, and I assist in a phone session.

Anne is an energy healer, intuitive, and spiritual teacher. She has walked the same path as her clients. Empowering women, she guides them to heal karmic patterns and dissolve deep wounds. They also transmute their darkness into Light.

Anne: *In my session with Lyn and Michael, I am going through a "Dragon Fire Initiation."*

Lyn: *Anne is fighting against the Divine Masculine.*

Anne: *My inner child wants to fight. As a young child, I experienced sexual abuse. My child pushes its legs out. It wants to stop other women from being abused.*

Lyn: *When a female or male child encounters abuse, they lose their 'Right to Be'. They also unconsciously take on the abuser's dark energy. You can clear this energy with intention and sound, such as Tibetan bells, crystal bells, or bowls.*

Anne: *I feel Divine Grace come through me when I talk to the schoolchildren I teach.* **Session Ended.**

Today, I understand the influence of my childhood. My father numbed his feelings and pain through alcohol. I am grateful I never succumbed to this addiction. However, I did into my thirties numb my feelings.

I learned from my mother's self-sacrifice and caretaking of those close to me.

I have since learned to nurture myself first, although I am still challenged. I tend to take on other people's energies, unaware of my desire to assist them.

Spiritual and Self-Growth

I recognize a pattern from my father. I swore as a teenager never to drink. Yet gradually, over seven years, I began drinking. In college, I would sit in my apartment on weekends. I would listen to music and drink Southern Comfort.

One day, a new meditation practice required no drinking. I quit. I did so for four years. After that, I no longer had a craving for alcohol.

It takes tremendous willpower to break such an addictive pattern. Over thirty years, I have become more aware of my inner pain and trauma.

I studied and applied various awareness and energy healing methods.

Through spiritual growth and higher consciousness, I have healed many pain patterns.

Self-growth and overcoming challenges remain an ongoing journey on this earth plane.

3 – How to Heal Your Wounded Inner Child

Embracing My Inner Child

For most of my life, my wounded child wanted to stay angry and rant at the injustices of the world or sink into the powerlessness of the victim.

With the help of my wife, Lyn, a gifted energy healer, I learned how to hold the emotions of my inner child rather than drowning in them or being trapped in anger.

I learned to embrace my child. By staying present with my feelings, they began to transform into peace. I do this more and more now. As an adult, I choose to take charge of my inner child.

The following is another client's experience with her inner child.

My wife, Lyn, and I Assisted in a Phone Session.

Alice grew up in an Eastern country where many families lack the basic necessities of life. She serves on many committees and supports humanity's interconnectedness.

Alice: *In my family, my mom demeaned me as a child. My father's only interest focused on making money. He never had any interest in who I was. I felt an ache in my heart.*

Lyn: *Alice, I am clearing your heart with energy. Alice, please give a verbal command to clear your husband's family from you.*

Your inner child wants to take care of everyone. You were energetically carrying your husband's family in your heart.
Session Ended.

Couples can take on the energy of their birth family. You can take on your father's or mother's lineage without knowing it. Their lives, including past lives, may affect you in the present day.

Inner Child: Your inner child always wants control of any situation. That is their nature until you, as the adult, discipline them. Who do you want in the driver's seat, you as the adult or your inner child? If you have constant drama, then that is the clue. Your child is in charge.

Heal Your Inner Child

"If you choose to heal your inner child, ultimately, what is important to realize is that the heart of self-love lies in loving, healing, and reparenting your inner child." ~ Evelyn Lim

Evelyn Lim, a life coach, writer, NLP practitioner, and an Intuitive Consultant, describes seven steps:

1. Understand your childhood programming.
2. Recognize repeated life patterns.
3. Acknowledge your pain.
4. Disengage in self-judgment.
5. Embrace the wounded child.
6. Practice courage.
7. Free yourself through forgiveness.

4 - How to Better Reparent Your Inner Child

The wounded inner child contaminates intimacy in relationships. He has no sense of his real, authentic self. ~ John Bradshaw, author of *Healing the Shame That Binds You*

As a teen boy, I suffered. I carried the same last name as my father. Everyone in my small town knew my father, the alcoholic. The shame weighed heavy on my shoulders.

Within my mind, I hobbled around bearing a wounded inner child. I felt low self-esteem or "less than" others.

Do you have a wounded inner child?

My wife and most of my clients have had a wounded inner child—also, most of my male friends.

The inner child lives in your subconscious with feelings of low self-esteem, shame, and trauma. My inner child is about five years old. Your child may be younger or older.

Reparenting/healing my inner child involved my adult self. As an adult, I had the choice to nurture my child. Eventually, healing transformed both our lives and resulted in a return to innocence for the child. Young children have an innocence and curiosity.

Wounding Before Birth

1. At conception, did you enter the womb already wounded?
   Did you experience more wounding in the womb? Was there wounding at birth or after birth? How did your father's and mother's family lineage affect you?

2. At conception, did you enter the womb already wounded? Many people come into the womb already wounded. The wounds come from previous lives.

3. Did you experience more wounding in the womb? Your mother carries her painful memories. These include feelings of anger, hurt, fear, etc. Any of these can influence a growing baby. These wounds may be physical, emotional, mental, or spiritual.

4. Was there wounding at birth or after birth? Difficulties at childbirth may occur.

How did your father's and mother's family lineage affect you? Your family lineage includes those members directly related. It also consists of those who lived before you.

I entered the womb wounded. Wounding also occurred after birth. My father's lineage had a strong effect. Subconscious beliefs influenced me, such as low esteem, shame, and trauma.

Your childhood consists of both positive and negative experiences. From this, you form conscious and unconscious beliefs.

Who is Your Wounded Inner Child?

You recognize your inner child through your body's feelings and emotions. Your child lives in your subconscious. Your wounded inner child shows itself when you become emotionally triggered. Your child may react and blame others.

My child carried a lot of anger. I also unknowingly took on my father's anger.

Does your child run your life instead of your adult self? Is your child in the driver's seat of a careening bus? A bus hurtling side to side down the street.

In Ann's experience, her child's fear of the destroyer occupied the driver's seat.

The following is Ann's experience of her inner child. My wife, Lyn, and I assisted in a phone session.

Anne works as an energy healer, intuitive, and spiritual teacher. She has walked the same path as her clients. Empowering women, she guides them to heal karmic patterns and dissolve deep wounds. Clients transmute their darkness into Light.

Anne: *In my session with Lyn and Michael, the old person is dying. I feel a lot of fear.*

Lyn: *I see a balance of energy coming in for you, Ann. It is a balance of Love and Power. Also, there is a destroyer aspect.*

The destroyer within you, Anne, wants to crush your husband. Your inner child, out of fear, wants to destroy something it does not understand.

Women have allowed men to crush the life out of them. Over time, each couple can learn to balance the other.

I will describe the Stillpoint. It balances. The Stillpoint is a place to cultivate your inner life. It is a spiritual meditative practice that assists with polarity within yourself.

Anne: *I realize I feel unappreciated by my husband. Then, I fall into the pit of the inner child victim. When I work with my clients, it brings up their polarity.*

Lyn: *Ann, breathe into your second chakra/belly. Now, breathe down the whole center point of your body. This is your* **center point** *or Stillpoint. You will feel peace at some point instead of chaos. Peace at the "Eye of the Tornado." Energy goes through your whole body.*

You can teach this to your five-year-old daughter.

If you are interested, get a meditator to teach you a Stillpoint Meditation. I describe the meditation in Chapter 6. **Session Ended.**

What Does Your Inner Child Feel?

- When does your child feel loved, recognized, and confident?
- Does he/she feel unheard, unloved, and unseen?
- Is your child feeling trapped, sad, and lonely?

A feeling of love or lack of love gets passed down through your family bloodline.

For most of my life, I bore the weight of my father's unworthiness. I came in feeling alone and unseen.

"We cannot heal what we cannot feel. So, without recovery, our toxic shame gets carried for generations." ~ John Bradshaw, author of Healing the Shame That Binds You

What Emotions and Feelings Does Your Inner Child Experience?

- Anger, hopelessness, hurt, rage, or sadness?
- Lack of love with anxieties, fears, and sorrow?
- Feeling unsafe and wanting to control every action?
- Low self-esteem?
- Powerless?
- Being emotionally "triggered" by situations or people?
- Wants to sabotage your success?

Pick one or more of the feelings your inner child experiences. Examine it more closely.

Did you know you have an inner family? They will assist in reparenting your inner child.

Your inner family includes the child, nurturer, sage/wise woman, and warrior/warrioress. With a healthy connection, your inner child feels safe within your psyche.

This inner family manifests in your outer relationships. When balanced and healthy, you have successful relationships.

Inner Family:

The inner nurturer ensures the child is heard and free to play within imaginary kingdoms. The inner sage translates the child's nonverbal communications, which are relayed to the inner warrior.

Is Your Inner Child Dysfunctional or Healthy?

Your child is also present in the teen years. The child/teen acts out.

Does your child "feel less than?"

As a teen, I hid in the shadows as a wallflower. I never acted out. Like many men, I wrestled with feeling "less than."

Dysfunctional Inner Child

- Lacks self-esteem; feels something is wrong with them.
- Strives to receive attention outside of themselves.
- Feels less than – see me – hear me.
- Constant mind chatter, wanting to figure everything out.
- Criticizes itself.
- Blames itself.
- Feels ashamed a lot.
- Wants to be in control.
- Does your child control and run your life instead of your adult self?

4 – How to Better Reparent Your Inner Child

Your child connects to your body and feelings. You need to re-parent your child. Most children have never experienced unconditional loving parenting. As you nurture your child, she/he begins to feel safe.

Healthy Child

- Expresses feelings and emotions.
- Enjoys living in the now moment.
- Feels safe and valued.
- Life force flows through the body.
- Lives with innocence and spontaneity.
- Plays and explores his/her environment.
- Radiates happiness and joy.

The following is a client's experience with her inner child. My wife, Lyn, and I assisted in a phone session.

Karen focuses daily on her Spiritual Growth. She has skills as a Light Worker and Sound Healer. The Universal Christ, Archangel Michael, Mother Mary, and Yogananda guide her. Karen calls on her guides to clear dark Entities that attempt to interfere with her. Spiritual empowerment is her goal.

Karen: *An orange entity interfered with me during my session with Lyn and Michael. I asked for help. None of my spiritual guides answered.*

Lyn: *Karen, take a deep breath. Take it all the way through your body. Let Divine Grace come into your body.*

Karen: *I feel peace.*

Lyn: *Karen, you have major fear in your second chakra, your belly. This fear affects your nervous system; the belly is where your inner child lives.*

Only ten percent of the fear is yours. Ask Mother Mary to smooth out your nervous system. You have had lifetimes of annihilation. It has left you vulnerable. Disincarnated spirits have followed you back in each lifetime. Michael and I are holding the Grace of the Divine Love of Mother Mary for you.

Karen: *I am connecting to the Divine Love of Mother Mary. In the name of Mother Mary, I Command all dark spirits to go into the Violet Fire Now. I feel an energy wave of fullness. I sense a lot of repairs in my body and energy field.* **Session Ended.**

The spiritual master, Saint Germain, holds the Violet Fire. This high-frequency light, when called upon, creates positive change for you. The Violet Fire dissolves negative energy.

Your inner child wants all the attention, all the time. As an adult, you need to discipline your child. Imagine a tree house at the eighth chakra, directly above your crown/head chakra. Send your child up there to play and relax.

When subconscious conflicts and patterns are apparent, your child heals. You then bypass your left brain. Trust your intuitive feelings when making decisions. A healthy child uses feelings as a guide for truth.

What activities does your inner child enjoy?

4 – How to Better Reparent Your Inner Child

Conclusion:

The unhealthy child engages in codependent behaviors. They use their power to manipulate. Dysfunction equals powerlessness.

Nothing heals a child's broken heart when unheard and misunderstood.

When healed, a child responds rather than reacts.

"We should talk to our child several times a day for healing to take place. The little child has been left alone for a long time, so we need to begin this practice right away. Go back to your inner child daily and listen for five or ten minutes, and healing will occur." ~ Thich Nhat Hanh, Buddhist Monk, author of *Listening to Your Inner Child: Art of Communicating*

Practice listening to your inner child every day.

5 - Do You Know Your Wounded Inner Child Needs Healing?

Consciousness is the core experience of our child within. It transcends our five senses, our co-dependent self. ~ Dr. Charles Whitfield, author of Healing the Child Within

What is Your Wounded Inner Child?

You may be unaware of your inner child, who lives within your subconscious mind. Many people carry wounding or pain in their bodies.

Did you grow up in a "troubled" home?

In some homes, parents argue and fight constantly.

Was your child stifled, unable to breathe?

Families may have oppression or depression weighing heavy over them like a pallor. It is difficult to breathe because of stress.

As a young child, did you ever feel neglected, afraid, or hurt? Did you feel you could express these feelings?

When a child feels afraid and unsafe, they stop expressing themselves. They fear they will be hurt.

Did you have a voice?

I felt alone all the time. Never did I think I could speak up. I had no idea of my feelings. If I did express, a part of me feared my father would yell or beat me.

I was unaware/unconscious. I had no sense that I had an inner child until my forties. Furthermore, I never knew my child was wounded. I had no idea that it could be healed. Even if I had wanted to, how would I heal this child?

I experienced significant codependency. In female relationships, my personal boundaries are enmeshed with my partner. I gave all of myself and my money away to please my partner. It took me half a lifetime to become conscious and heal codependency.

If you have emotional reliance on a partner, find help. Talk to a friend, find a codependence therapist, or a recovery group.

How Do You Recognize the Signs Your Child Needs Healing? As an adult, do you experience:

- Repeated fear of intimacy, mistrust, or shame?
- Feeling unlovable or less than?
- Desire to please others?
- Issues with authority?
- Judgment or criticism of yourself or others?

- Intense anger?
- Feelings of isolation?
- Repeated patterns of conflict?
- Failed relationships?
- Repeating emotional reactions to people or events?

I experienced all the above signs. My child still gets angry and desires to please others. I then connect with my adult self and set boundaries with the child.

The signs can or show a wounded inner child asking for healing.

Healing Your Wounded Inner Child. Your wounded child splits off. Disconnects because of family trauma.

As I said earlier, you may have felt afraid, hurt, or abandoned.

Did you feel afraid to express these feelings in your family? These severed parts contain positive qualities of truth, love, or courage.

As an adult, do you search outside yourself for love from others?

When will you decide to do something about your pain and suffering?

When someone pushes your emotional buttons, do you react from memories? If your reaction is energetic, this means old wounds have been activated.

What if you could stay in the present moment with your feelings?

"To be a truly alive, loving adult, we must first feel the pain of our past. Accept the pain, know the pain, and be with the pain without jumping to defense or acting out." ~ John Bradshaw, author of *Homecoming*

As a child, do/did you experience powerlessness? As an adult, you can stop being a victim. You can take back your power. Or you can continue blaming your parents for their imperfections.

Loving Parent

You can now decide to be a loving parent—the parent you never had. You can nurture your inner child. Learn to hear the inner voice of your child. Or you can continue to criticize your inner child.

Do you call yourself stupid or worthless? Then you remain an abuser and neglectful like your parents.

How can you begin to connect with your inner child?

Ask inwardly when your emotional buttons get pushed. How old am I feeling now? Use your intuition. Listen for the first answer you get. You may get four, five, six, or seven years old, etc.

Methods to Heal Your Inner Child

To open communications with your child:

- Journal daily.

5 – Do You Know Your Wounded Inner Child Needs Healing?

- Ask questions of your child.
- Write down any thoughts that occur without censoring in any way.
- Use your non-dominant hand, i.e., the one you never write with.
- Paint like a child.
- Childlike drawing or doodling.
- Walking in nature barefoot.
- Physical activity of any kind your child enjoys.
- Have therapy sessions with a therapist, an energy healer, or someone who has done their emotional healing.
- Soul Retrieval of split-off child aspects. When a person experiences trauma, part of themselves can separate. A skilled healer or shaman connects and brings that part back to the body.

Do some of the above activities weekly. When you make a promise, follow through so your child can develop trust and feel loved.

Will you choose to become a loving parent to your inner child?

Have you ever wondered why your life never gets better?

If your child never has the chance to heal, you will recreate the pain and suffering from your child's wounds. You do this continually and unconsciously.

This child will continue, as it has in the past, to run your life with its emotional trauma and wounds.

Healing our inner child creates a solid foundation for strong self-esteem.

If you have a wounded inner child, seek help. Talk to a friend, or find an inner child therapist, skilled healer, or shaman.

The following is a client's experience of healing their wounded inner child. My wife, Lyn, and I assisted in a phone session.

Laura describes herself as an author, healer, professor, and teacher. She assists her clients in recovery from burnout and trauma.

Laura: *In my session with Lyn and Michael, I explained how I allow other people's judgments to destroy trust in myself. My inner child desires to be seen so very much.*

Lyn: *Laura, if you are familiar with them, connect with Green Tara and Archangel Michael. They have come to help you.*

Laura: *My third eye chakra, throat, and heart are clearing stuck energy.*

Now, I feel intense fear in my first chakra at my tailbone. A black blob of dread just transformed. I saw Saint Germain send it to Violet Fire.

Lyn: *Your inner child lives primarily in your second chakra/belly. The fear transmuted at the tailbone. I recommend, chanting the Green Tara mantra daily as homework. It aligns you with* *compassion for yourself and courage. Chanting Om Tare Tuttare Ture Soha relieves you of suffering. Go to YouTube to hear the pronunciation.*

Also, use the Violet Flame Mantra by Saint Germain for transmuting your personal and planetary past errors in thought, feeling, and action. I AM a Being of Violet Fire. I AM the Purity God Desires. **Session Ended.**

Inner Child Books

Read and apply the methods of:

Healing the Child Within by Charles Whitfield.

Homecoming: Reclaiming and Championing Your Inner Child by John Bradshaw.

Inner Child Therapy

"If you feel alone, empty, anxious, depressed, hurt, angry, jealous, sad, fearful, guilty, or shamed, you are abandoning yourself." ~ Dr. Margaret Paul, Ph.D. Psychology, author of *Inner Bonding: Becoming a Loving Adult to Your Inner Child*

A feeling of abandonment as a child creates our first major wound. This abandonment can manifest as loneliness alone or in groups. You can feel unseen by your parents, siblings, or peers. This feeling becomes active in our inner child and taints all our relationships.

Go inside yourself and become aware of how your inner child feels. Do you feel overwhelmed, out of control, lost, little, lonely, or plain sick and tired? These feelings tell us our inner child needs attention.

Take a breath and imagine connecting with your child within you.

Imagine talking to your inner child and asking them:

- What do you feel?
- What do you need?
- What would you like to do?

The minute we become aware and ask, the energy starts to move. For example, notice at this moment that you feel unsafe. Be aware of what would help you feel safe. Imagine giving that to yourself. Take responsibility for your own needs. Taking action supports both you and your inner child's growth.

The following is another client's experience of healing their childhood abuse. Your childhood wounds affect your adult self. My wife, Lyn, and I assisted in a phone session.

Linda describes herself as a professor. She intends to reduce distress, injury, and suffering for clients in her field.

Linda: *In my session with Lyn and Michael, we looked at an injury in my left hip. It resulted in a man grabbing my purse, and I fell. I still feel the shock in my hip.*

My body holds abuse as a young child. My mother yelled at me. I felt small. If I made any noise, my mother would whack me. She controlled me this way.

I later understood my mother's family had a lineage of abuse.

Lyn: *Linda, you named the issue. The abuse goes back a long way in time. Now, I can call in Divine Grace to heal.*

Linda, you were blamed for nothing you did. Now connect with your Divine I AM. This dissolves your programming at birth. Only fifteen percent is your anger. The anger is releasing now. You are claiming your "Right to Be."

When you experience any emotions, only a percentage is yours. The rest is the emotion of collective humanity. Sense intuitively how much is yours. It will be the first number that comes to you. Then clear that. You use intent plus sound. Tibetan bells or crystal bells or bowls work.

Your father and mother's lineage affects you. For example, a grandmother or great-grandmother may have had lung issues. You or your child may inherit similar challenges.

Your "Right to Be" refers to Who You Are at your deepest essence. It connects with your Divine I AM.

Conclusion:

- The wounds I mentioned have the gift of connection within them. Hold your inner child. Then, imagine holding yourself tenderly.

- Honor your pain. Allow the Light of the Divine, in whatever way this comes to you. The Divine shines upon the wound until it is ready to dissolve. Complete surrender; no forcing anything. This may take some time, days, or weeks.

- Do you feel shame about your wounds and keep them hidden? By connecting with your wounds and allowing Divine Light, healing occurs. Healing emotional abuse also occurs.

- All this strengthens your central core, the foundation of your being. You can imagine this as a pillar of golden light. It aligns through the center of our body from head to toe.

Ponder This: Cathryn L. Taylor writes in *The Inner Child Workbook,* "*The inner child embodies the characteristics of the innocent part of the self. What you do not master in childhood reappears in your adult lives. It shows up as inappropriate responses to people, places, or things.*"

6 - Meditations to Better Heal Your Inner Child Trauma

What is Your Pain Body? My inner child felt a lot of pain growing up. From childhood on, pain grows.
~ Eckhart Tolle, author of The Power of Now

What is the Pain Body?

Eckhart Tolle calls the buildup of pain the "pain body." He describes the pain-body as an energy field of old, very much alive emotion. It lives in most humans. On the other hand, your pain-body challenges you to grow in higher consciousness.

Tolle says the pain takes many forms, such as blame, drama, and fear.

Pain also includes hate, hurt, and physical illness. Any emotional pain experience strengthens your pain body. Your pain body thrives on negative thinking and drama. Any negative emotion not faced as it arises, never dissolves. It leaves behind a remnant of pain.

Do you assume your pain is who you are?

Pain is part of being human. It is impossible to escape the pain. Does pain involve how your father or mother treated you?

You may feel low esteem or turn to drugs or alcohol because your father ignored you. Also, you may enter unhealthy relationships.

Most of my female clients feel unloved and unseen by their mothers. Their mother experienced a lack of love growing up.

Do you build a story around your trauma of pain?

I built a story and kept repeating it for decades. My inner child felt overwhelmed, out of control, lost, little, lonely, and fatigued. My child always craved attention.

What Are Some Signs of Childhood Trauma?

"Trauma is a psychic wound that hardens you. That then interferes with your ability to grow and develop. It pains you, and now you're acting out of pain. It induces fear, and now you're acting out of fear." ~ Gabor Mate, M.D.

Inner Child

- Fights, manipulates, and resists.
- Wants to control.
- Be stubborn.
- Gets angry.
- Often, the child wants to wallow in suffering/poor me.

- Often, the child feels unworthy, unloved, unrecognized.
- The child in a pit of suffering will never release suffering.

My child always resists. He is stubborn. For three years, he sunk into the pit daily. I felt it. So, I learned to recognize the feeling. I no longer remain in the pit. My adult takes charge.

Adult Assist Child Heal Trauma

- The child has no awareness of how to climb out of the pit of suffering.
- The adult never gives in to the child.
- Set strong boundaries.
- The child often resists receiving love.
- Encourage the child to let go.

"The pain-body fears the light of your consciousness. It is afraid that you will discover it. Its survival depends on your continuing to unconsciously identify with it." ~ Eckhart Tolle, author of *The Power of Now*

Shifting Awareness from Outer to Inner

Through meditation, I learned to shift my thoughts. I focused on feelings in my body. Noticing the tension and stuck energy opened a flow and ease. Then healing began. This took constant practice and required shifting my conscious awareness to inside my body.

I had the choice of ongoing suffering or some discomfort at the moment. By paying attention to the stuck energy, my attitude shifted.

I became present to my body in a new way.

I stopped figuring out and talking about my challenges. As an observer, I avoided getting lost in the discomfort. I opened compassion for myself.

My inner child had frozen in trauma for a long time.

- Where are you stuck in your life? Career, finances, or
- relationships? Your frozen inner child waits for you as the adult to free it.
- Remember yourself as a child. See an image of your child as a little boy or girl.
- Imagine your adult consciousness holding your child. This creates a link to your Higher Consciousness. The following mediations show this.

Meditations to Heal Your Inner Child Trauma

Meditation 1 – Stillness Meditation

Stillness Meditation (to deal with voices in mind, critical voices/self-judgment)

Essentially, you sit in a quiet environment and clear your mind of all thoughts.

Focus on the breath entering and leaving your body. When you feel your mind drift, you come back to your breath.

Practiced consistently, this meditation helps you stay present in daily life.

Notice your mind chatter. You are thinking about the past or the future.

Thinking about the past involves critical thoughts or replaying failures. Also, what could you have done differently?

For many years, I have done transformational land journeys in Sedona. I taught most clients the Stillness Meditation out on the land.

Thinking about the future includes worrying about what may or may not happen.

Choose to Come into the Present Moment

- Focus on your breath and body.
- Breathe into the center of your body.
- Take a deep breath all the way down into your belly. Your belly will expand out. If necessary, put your hand on your belly.
- Keep staying in the present and breathing for five minutes or so. If your mind strays to the past or future, bring it back.
- If you have an active mind, it is impossible to stop thinking.

The method requires a constant return to the present and the breath. With daily practice, you have more space without thought.

Focus on the breath and the body during your practice. You pull yourself out of the stress and worries about tomorrow. Now, you root yourself firmly into the present moment.

Meditation 2 – Dr. Hew Len Ho'oponopono Inner Child Meditation

Ho'oponopono is Hawaiian for to make things right. It teaches love and forgiveness.

In this meditation, Hew Len guides you to heal your inner child as an adult.

See the four steps:

1. Repentance – SAY: I'M SORRY.
2. Ask Forgiveness – SAY: PLEASE FORGIVE ME.
3. Gratitude – SAY: THANK YOU.
4. Love – SAY: I LOVE YOU.

Dr. Hew Len cured an entire ward of criminally mentally ill patients. It took four years. He used the ancient Hawaiian healing method of Ho'oponopono.

Dr. Hew Len says that Ho'oponopono is the process of saying to The Divine: "I love you" (unification), "I'm sorry" (repentance), "Please forgive me" (forgiveness), and "Thank you" (transmutation).

Do this meditation daily until you begin to feel the effects. I recommend this method to clients.

"Ho'oponopono|Inner Child Guided Meditation" by Hew Len on YouTube.

Meditation 3 – Tree House Inner Child Meditation.

My wife and I have guided phone clients in this meditation for years. It involves both your inner child and adult.

A tree house is a platform above ground. Build it around the trunk of a tree. It is at your 8th chakra—this chakra is about 1/2 vertical hand width above your head.

The following includes a client's experience of Tree House Inner Child Meditation. It is also the client's experience of inner child healing.

Linda describes herself as a professor. She intends to reduce distress, injury, and suffering for clients in her field.

My wife, Lyn, and I assisted in a phone session.

Linda: *My inner child is tired of holding everything together, particularly the relationship between my boyfriend and me. My mother always blamed me if anything went wrong. She wanted to take all the love for herself.*

Lyn: *Be vulnerable and allow your boyfriend to cherish you.*

Linda: It is difficult to be patient with my boyfriend.

Lyn: *Linda, take your inner child to the Tree House. It is at the eighth chakra above your head. Your little girl can relax there. Now imagine the Divine cherishing you.*

Linda: *I feel bliss. It is incredible.*

Lyn: *I see a lot of untwisting in your stomach area. You have learned a lot about accepting being cherished.* **Session Ends.**

Meditation 4: Inner Child Preparation

- You, as the adult, connect with your child below your belly button. Ask the child when ready to climb up to the 8th chakra. Climb up the ladder, rope, elevator, etc.

- As the child climbs up the body, experience what area the child is at. Wait until the child reaches the 8th chakra.
- Ask the child to climb into a safe place: the tree house.
- Suggest the child taste Divine love when it is ready. If the child likes it, keep tasting it. The Divine is Grace. It is only received once you trust the Divine. Surrender/let go one hundred percent.
- Your Adult self may feel/experience energy through and down the body. The Adult may see Light in the body or feel lighter.
- If you have mind chatter, invite the child back to the 8th chakra. If the child is feeling emotions, invite the child back to the 8th chakra.

Your child reveals itself through your mind and emotions.

Meditation 5: Adult Meditation

- You, as the adult, connect to the Divine at the 8th chakra. The 8th chakra is one vertical hand width above your head.
- Then, start at the crown and breathe down each body part. This includes the third eye/middle of the head, throat, heart/center of the chest, stomach, below the belly button, and tailbone.

6 – Meditation to Better Heal Your Inner Child Trauma

- Take your time with each breath. Continue at each area until stuck energy releases. You will feel more flow.
- Then, breathe into the center of Earth. Energy now travels back up the body to the crown.
- The energy spirals back to Divine and down again.

After this meditation, your child returns to the second chakra/belly. The child naturally lives in the belly. In the long run, as the child heals, it returns to more innocence, creativity, and joy.

7 - How to Heal Your Wounded, Suffering Inner Child

Vulnerability is the core of shame and fear and our struggle for worthiness. It appears that it's also the birthplace of the joy of creativity. ~ Brene Brown, author of *The Power of Vulnerability*

I will describe five aspects of your inner child. I show you ways of healing your suffering child. Encourage your child to begin feeling vulnerable. Fear is overcome.

"The magic, the wonder, the mystery, and the innocence of a child's heart are the seeds of creativity that will heal the world." ~ Michael Jackson

Four Inner Child Aspects

1. **King/Queen** – Tantrum Behavior
   - You may know adults who refuse to accept "No" from their partner. The partner "walks on eggshells." They give in out of fear of the partner's emotional tantrum.

- You know children who cry or scream when their demands are unmet. They throw themselves on the ground.
- Your inner child can do the same inside you. Your inner child wants to rule the household or his/her kingdom.
- Your inner child tests your ability to establish strong boundaries with love.

Healing Tantrum Behavior

Overcoming Fear of Setting Healthy Boundaries

You may feel anger or fear arising around creating boundaries.

- Become aware of your feelings.
- Breathe or take a quick time out.
- Now, come back to your feelings.
- Respond now from a centered place and set the boundary.

You may have to walk away when a physical child "acts out." Then, the child gets no attention for this behavior. The above also applies to your inner child.

2. Manipulator - Controller

A child tricks adults into giving it what it wants. A child wants what it wants when it wants it. Your inner child acts the same way. On an inner level, imagine talking to your inner child. Ask them what they want. You can also use a journal to allow your child to communicate. Your inner child has no training in receiving and giving.

Healing the Manipulator - Controller

- Teach your inner child, as the adult, you take charge.
- Never allow your child to run/ruin your life.

Your controller fears losing control. Do you fear showing vulnerability?

3. Good Boy/Girl – Jokester/Clown

These children/inner children act quiet and compliant. They make jokes and clown around. These children avoid conflict. They want to make everyone happy, ignoring their feelings and needs.

Your suffering child desires recognition. You may know adults who have the above behavior. Their inner child bends backward to please others. They seek approval in unhealthy ways. This behavior shows your codependency.

Healing the Jokester/Clown

The trauma of your inner child requires steps toward Codependency Recovery.

Codependency

1. Codependency results from childhood trauma.
2. As an addiction, you may feel less than others.
3. You have poor boundaries.
4. Your own needs and feelings suffer.
5. Do you constantly please everyone else?
6. Does your inner child take on over-responsibility for others?

4. **Rebel – Acting Out**
   - The rebel inner child acts out in adult relationships. Like children, teenagers also rebel. Rebels have no desire to deal with authority.
   - They do what they want. They answer truthfully to no adult.
   - Does your inner child rebel against your adult? The most common response is "F" YOU!
   - The "Little You" has no desire to hear "NO" or experience change. It only knows resistance. Stuck in your traumatic childhood patterns, we never grow emotionally.

Healing the Rebel
   - Communicate – Imagine talking directly to your inner child.
   - Discover her/his feelings and fears. Encourage your child to begin feeling vulnerable, bit by bit.
   - When you open your defiant contracted self, suffering lessens.
   - Opening to vulnerability invites more life to enter.

Listen to *Power of Vulnerability* by Brene Brown.

Truth: How to Feel Better

Growing up in the Western world, you are taught to avoid showing any emotions. So, when feelings begin overtaking you, you stop breathing and apologize for feeling. As a result, your inner child, the emotional part of you, lives with its wounds and suffers.

Emotions, or E for energy in motion, want to express themselves naturally through your body. When you stop the flow of these feelings, they gather and become trapped in different parts of your body and your inner child.

Repressed and suppressed over periods of time, Emotions can develop into physical conditions—examples such as heart disease or cancer etc.

What is the Truth About Feelings?

1. Denying your childhood emotional wounds will not make them magically disappear. As I said earlier, emotions manifest as energy. Suppression causes them to stay trapped in your body and your inner child. Pressure builds until you explode outward or the energy implodes inward. PTSD represents emotional trauma trapped in the bodies of war survivors.

2. You can suppress your feelings through addictions like alcohol and drugs. It can also be over-exercising, food, religion, sex, work, or television. You run away from your feelings because of the terror of facing them. You become overwhelmed or fear losing control. Then, the emotional wounds of your childhood suffered by your inner child will run through your life. The child, rather than the adult, sits in the driver's seat of your life. How often as an adult have you felt like a young child? This is your inner child.

3. You can receive "truth" about feelings in two different ways.

1. Intuitive Emotional Truth comes from your higher self or soul. It reveals the best choices for you to follow for your highest personal growth.
2. Personality Emotional Truth, which comes from a reaction of your inner child. A reaction based on wounds from past situations. You react in a knee-jerk way as an angry, scared, or powerless child. This child is three, five, or seven years old, etc. As an adult, you could respond as you feel in the present moment.

4. Do you unconsciously attract relationships reflecting your unhealed inner child/childhood wounds? For example, do you attract partners who are unable to love? They criticize rather than support you. Do you continue attracting these unhealthy relationships? Thus, you confirm your lack of lovability. These patterns continue until you choose to begin healing your inner child's wounds.

5. Will you continue feeling a hole in your soul until you break down and surrender completely? Then Divine Grace can infuse you. This assists in dissolving and healing your wounds. Any type of addiction, alcohol, codependency, drugs, etc. indicates a hole in your soul. This results in isolation, loneliness, and separation.

Do You Want to Feel Better?

What changes will you make in your life to feel better? What will you do to heal your inner child and your adult self?

Tips: Healing Your Inner Child Feelings

- Connect with your feelings to begin to release and heal.

- Talk to trusted friends, journal, draw, or paint your feelings to feel and express them in healthy ways.

- Connect with and allow your inner child to talk to you about what it needs. Let it journal by writing with your non-dominant hand. Allow free expression without interference from your mind or judgments.

- Choose to look at the repetitive painful patterns of your unsuccessful relationships. Find a therapist or energy healer who has done their emotional healing. Have them assist you in healing your inner child.

- To receive Divine Grace, you must surrender your mind's fears and the suffering of what you believe to be reality or truth.

As the spiritual teacher Yogananda says, *"All surrendering love draws His Grace. Divine Grace can dissolve any emotions standing in the way of our healing when we are ready."*

A Few Books for Healing Inner Child Feelings

Focusing by Eugene Gendlin – releases tension and psychological stress.

The Emotion Code by Bradley Nelson is a simple way to clear trapped emotions.

Emotional Health. The Secret for Freedom from Drama, Trauma, and Pain by Michael David Lawrience. Practical methods to release your physical and emotional chronic pain. Also, releasing suffering and emotional stress.

8 – Three Practical Steps for Healing Your Victim Inner Child

Before you judge me, try hard to love me. Look within your heart, then ask. Have you seen my Childhood? It's been my fate to compensate for the Childhood I've never known. ~ Michael Jackson, Song Childhood Inner Child Healing

Like Jackson, I have had to compensate for my childhood, for the trauma.

As a performer, Michael had to work rather than be a child. He lost his childhood.

The clients I work with deal with healing their inner child. This occurs when they are ready, and it also takes time to heal the patterns.

Do you have an inner child victim? Is your inner child victim caught in early childhood trauma?

Michael: *Like many, I suffered from the above. As a child, I seldom felt loved. As an adult, I felt afraid, hyper-vigilant, and unsafe.*

Inner Child

- Inner child healing means caring for yourself, so the things of the past no longer hurt you.
- You stop feeding a "poor me" mentality.
- Does the outer story of your adult life reflect the inside story of your wounded child?
- Do you hold dysfunctional stories of your childhood?
- Are your relationships based on what you learned from your parents?

Inner Child Victim

My child victim feels unloved. He yearns for people to hear him. Also, he wants love and others to see him.

Michael: *I struggled feeling like a victim for most of my life. For half my life, I remained unaware of being a victim. On a subconscious level, the victim influenced my life. This means my child controlled and ran my life.*

In my seventies, for three years, daily, the victim child would raise its head. I would feel a loss of energy and fatigue. This signaled I had fallen into the pit of a victim.

My wife pointed this out to me. I begin to notice the signal: fatigue. Then, I knew my child had sunk into the victim.

What is a victim pit? The victim sinks deep into the ground. This swamp reacts to his/her struggle. It becomes thick like molasses. As the victim thrashes around, they get more stuck.

Why I Lived Often in the Victim Pit

Michael: *Recently, I became aware of the pit as my alcoholic father's emotional body. Our emotional body consists of the sum total of all our negative and positive emotions. I am, like most people, also a codependent. A codependent always wants to help others.*

I wanted to help my father, even though unaware of this. Second, my nature is to help others."

As an Energy Healer, I show clients how to heal themselves. This is part of my service to Humanity. It is who I am. I cannot help myself climb out when I am in the pit.

It would help if you chose to come out of your pit. In the pit, you remain unable to receive Divine Grace. Divine Grace, which comes as your connection to a Higher Source. This requires the complete surrender of your inner child wanting to control everything. It also means total surrender of your personality self.

How Does the Child Get Out of the Victim Pit?

This year, my wife developed a system for working with a client's inner child. We use it a lot. I will describe it. You can use it for yourself and your inner child.

Your child lives in the second chakra, below the belly button. Check in with your child. What is your child doing or feeling? When they are ready, invite them to climb the tree house. Your child has its way of going up.

I discovered that when my child is in the pit, he responds when I, as the adult, offer my hand to him. He grabs a hold until we are at the tree house. I have him then look up into the blue sky above. He loves looking into the infinite sky and connecting to the beauty of nature around him.

The following is a client's experience of her journey of spiritual growth.

My wife and I work together as Energy Healers. We work over the phone with clients.

The following is Melinda's experience of her Victim Inner Child. My wife, Lyn, and I assisted in a phone session. Lyn has the gift of seeing and feeling the energy in a client's body. I hold the energy for the client with Lyn.

Melinda has been on a path of self-healing for years.

Melinda describes her practice. She meditates, tuning deeply into herself. Diving into her intuitive mind, she receives higher conscious awareness.

Melinda: *I have received hundreds of hours of training in counseling and energy healing. I also have trained in meditation and kundalini yoga. Daily meditation keeps me centered.*

In my session with Lyn and Michael, my inner child, and I, as an adult, felt fatigued.

Lyn: *Melinda, feel the fatigue in your throat, heart, lungs, and large intestine. You're picking up on your inner child's trauma.*

You have been in the death cycle. Your body's losing energy. Let go of the fatigue. Send it into the Violet Fire.

Breathe in Life. You teach kundalini. Connect with your kundalini. Breathe it through your whole body from your head to feet."

Melinda: *I feel more energy.*

Lyn: *Your large intestine is holding a lot of resentment. You have resistance to Life. Breathe through your whole body. Now, consciously choose Life.*

In your subconscious, you had chosen death. Your inner child connects to the subconscious. Many people live most of their lives in their subconscious or inner child.

Melinda: *I am breathing Life into my whole body now.*

Lyn: Invite your child to climb into a tree house at the 8th chakra above your head. **Session Ended.**

Kundalini life force lies coiled at the base of the spine until aroused. When it travels through the body, at the head, you may feel peace.

Violet Fire: Violet Flame Mantra by Saint Germain. It transmutes personal and planetary past errors in thought, feeling, and action. I AM a Being of Violet Fire. I AM the Purity God Desires.

What Does Your Child Respond To?

Your child climbs up your body. They climb to the seventh chakra/crown at the top of your head. Next, the child can climb into the tree house above your head.

A tree house is a platform above ground. Build it around the trunk of a tree. It is at your 8th chakra—about 1/2 vertical hand width above your head.

Then, when they are ready, have the child go to the 8th chakra. This chakra aligns about a vertical hand width above the crown. Invite your child to climb into a tree house at the 8th chakra. Have them sit in the house with their feet pulled up. When they are ready, invite them to breathe in the love from the Divine.

The Divine is your connection to the Higher Self or Spiritual Self. You may connect to an angel or archangel like Michael. Your connection may be Mother Mary or the Divine, etc.

Richard Rudd, author of *The Gene Keys*, wrote a guide for 64 victim patterns.

As you move into higher consciousness, you go from Shadow to Gift and finally Siddha or divine gift. He describes Awareness, Compassion, and Transformation.

To Heal Your Inner Child Requires

1. Awareness.
2. Compassion.
3. Transformation.

Awareness

- Notice details when you fall into the inner victim child.
- What event occurred? (Conflict with a partner)
- What did you feel? (Anger or loss of energy)

- What thoughts did you have? (e.g., I am never heard, or I better just be quiet)

Compassion

- Be patient with yourself. (It takes time.)
- Accept and embrace your shadow (a part of your subconscious).
- Imagine holding it like a small child. This is your inner child.
- Notice the repeating emotions and beliefs that give the victim/shadow life.

Transformation

- Call in the Divine Light/Higher Power or the Gift related to the victim/shadow.
- Notice where you feel the shadow sensations in your body.
- Focus your attention and keep breathing into that area, i.e., your belly.
- Stay focused and breathing until you notice some change.

Repeat the three tools each time the victim/shadow appears. See More: Expanded details for dissolving victim patterns.

Awareness, Compassion, Transformation, ACT. Use the tools to take action.

Use a notebook and write your answers in it.

It took me a long time to gain Awareness of my victim. I discovered Compassion and Transformation later.

"To take good care of ourselves, we must go back and take care of the wounded child inside of us. Practice going back to your wounded child every day." ~Thích Nhat Hạnh, author of *Anger: Wisdom for Cooling the Flames*

More Resources for Healing the Victim Child:

The Gene Keys. Get a Your Free Gene Keys Profile by Richard Rudd

Peter Levine pioneered Somatic Experiencing Therapy. This healing process locates and moves trauma out of the body, repatterning the nervous system. Contact a therapist to release stress from your body.

It Didn't Start with You by Mark Wolynn, you can shift the painful childhood parts you inherited from your family. Read the book and answer the questions.

9 - Energy Healing to Heal Your Wounded Inner Child

Someday, the medical profession will wake up. They will realize that unresolved emotional issues are the main cause of 85% of all illnesses. ~ Dr. Eric Robins, MD, *The Tapping Solution*

As an adult, do you sometimes feel like an unloved child? I have.

What is Energy Healing?

Energy Healing has value for emotional healing and spiritual transformation. Also, I use it to heal the inner child with clients.

I have practiced Energy Healing for thirty years. In the beginning, I taught my system for four years. When applied to myself it has transformed my life.

As an adult, your inner child lives within you. Aspects of your child split off because of childhood trauma.

Was your child ridiculed or called names by other kids? Did you suffer abuse by adults?

Your inner child's nature consists of negative and positive childhood experiences, a truck load of emotions, and possibly low self-worth.

The inner child lies trapped between the ages of birth and adolescence.

Here is a client, Liam, who experienced his trauma at age three of his inner child. He locked up his emotions. It felt unsafe at three to trust them.

Inner Child Trauma

Liam: *I started therapy as I grieved the loss of my first love. One day, my therapist said, "I want to commend you." I think it is time now to go into deeper work.*

Great, let's go into my childhood trauma. Let's see where the healing takes us.

This was my second phase of intense talk therapy. The therapist asked me to ask my mom. When did I start to control my emotions?

My mom shared the following story: Liam had a yogi bear teddy at three. They were inseparable. Liam took the teddy everywhere, and he slept with him at night.

One night, as my mom put me to bed, she asked, where is Teddy?

I said he was gone.

My mom asked where did he go?

I said away. I don't need him anymore.

Energy Healing for Your Inner Child

An Energy Healer may touch your body. You may be fully clothed on a massage table. You may also sit in the healer's office or be on the phone.

The healer holds a sacred, safe space for you. This can be in person, over the phone, or at a distance. The healer discusses and decides what core issues you want to focus on. You recall what people and events pushed your emotional buttons recently. Then, set your intent for healing.

Healing occurs for emotional abuse and stress. It can dissolve the emotional causes behind most physical pain.

Energy Healing connects to your body and energy centers (chakras).

It addresses emotions and conscious and subconscious thoughts. The healing also connects you to your soul and Divine self.

The Divine energy flows through the healer, who has to have developed spiritually. They surrender and allow the Divine to perform the healing. You, as the client, breathe throughout. Feel the sensations in your body.

As you relax, congestion and pain lessen. Eventually, you may feel relaxation, calm, peace, etc.

The secret lies in surrender. Surrender to the Divine/Higher Power.

When you surrender, then Divine Grace/Love enters.

As you connect to your higher consciousness, all Divine beings assist. These include Angels, Archangels, Spiritual Masters, and your individual Divine Presence.

"Only the Hand of God Can remove the burdens of your heart."
~ Rumi, Islamic Mystic

"God picks up the reed-flute world and blows. Each note is a need coming through one of us, a passion, a longing pain. Remember the lips where the wind-breath originated, and let your note be clear. Don't try to end it. Be your note." ~ Rumi

According to Rumi, you and I serve as hollow flutes for the Divine.

Energy Healing for Your Inner Child Continued

As an Energy Healer, I learned how to bring healing energy from the Divine Source through my being. This energy enters into you as the client. I also encourage you to develop that ability during the session.

Psychological understanding and energy healing combine to heal your abused inner child. Soul retrieval may also be necessary to regain your inner child's lost parts. The child has split off because of trauma.

As I said, find someone who has done their emotional healing. They also understand the workings of the inner child. You trust them.

During the session, stay present in the moment. Notice sensations in your body as energy flows into you. As an abuse survivor, you may feel little or numb in parts of your body. Knowing these feelings may show you have shut down sensations in these parts because of trauma.

Energy begins to unfreeze the trauma and trapped emotions in these areas. You will begin to feel more. Pain may temporarily increase as it releases. You may feel an increase in heat, cold, or energy sensations. This occurs in different parts as the energy healing progresses. Different emotions may arise, such as anger, fear, or rage.

During an energy healing session, stay present with your body's sensations and whatever emotions emerge.

The only way out of your trauma lies through feeling your feelings. Your way out is through the fear and pain. The other choice is to continue living with the pain.

The trauma and abuse your inner child suffered for years stays trapped in the physical body. It takes time and many energy healing sessions to heal each core issue of abuse.

If ignored, your child will hide in a corner of your psyche. He/she does this until something triggers the pain again. Their emotional reaction can sabotage your success. A child's subconscious intent differs from your conscious intent.

Three Energy Centers Where the Child Lives

The first three energy centers (chakras) connect to our body: the tailbone, below the belly button, and the abdomen under the ribcage. These centers may hold a great deal of pain, physical and emotional. They carry your fears, anxieties, and sorrow.

These make up the life of an unloved child. As the inner child heals, your heart opens. You reach out to others more with loving arms.

As an adult, your inner child yearns for you to hear and love them. You may choose to continue to ignore the emotional part of your child. Then, it will run your life on a subconscious level. You could call this, "Hell on Wheels".

You always have a choice. You can continue to react, keep doing the same thing repeatedly, and expect different results. Or you can choose self-growth and higher consciousness.

Healing Environment

- In your healing, seek an environment of unconditional love.
- When you walk through the door of an energy healer, you feel an air of nurturing.
- Feel safe as if wrapped in the arms of a loving mother.
- When your inner child feels safe, fears lift.
- The child may move into higher levels of joy.
- Your unloved child begins to feel Divine Love.
- The child opens in innocence and childlike wonderment to all life.
- Your life magnetizes happiness, health, and success.

"As traumatized children, we always dreamed that someone would come and save us. We never dreamed that it would, in fact, be ourselves as adults." ~ Alice Little, author of *Narcissistic Abuse Truths*

The following is a client's experience of her journey of spiritual growth and healing her wounded inner child.

Anne is an energy healer, intuitive, and spiritual teacher. She has walked the same path as her clients. Empowering women, she guides them to heal karmic patterns and dissolve deep inner child wounds. They also transmute their darkness into Light.

Anne: *In my session with Lyn and Michael, they assisted me in healing my wounded inner child. Also, they helped me to understand the wounding.*

I have had a lot of past lives. My child never felt worthy enough. The child lived in terror.

Lyn: *Anne, you are facing the issue of power. Your inner child needs to take a back seat. Otherwise, your child and adult will be at war with each other. The child will sabotage the healing process. She wants recognition. More than anything, your child wants love.*

Anne: *I am seeking unconditional love for my inner child. As a child, I never felt unconditional love from my mother. My mother wounded herself and wanted all the love for herself. She never wrapped her arms around me. I never felt safe. Is there a way I no longer have to feel this childhood pain?*

Lyn: *Connect with your concept of the Divine/Higher Self. This is also known as the I AM. The I AM is your individual spark of the Divine.*

Connect with intent to your I AM. Breathe it down to the top of your head. Then, breathe it into every part of your body. Bring the breath to the middle of your forehead, throat, heart, stomach, belly, and finally, your feet. Now breathe the I AM down into the center of the Earth. Then breathe all the way back up your whole body to the Divine.

Anne: *I have some sense of Peace in my body.* **Session Ended.**

It takes continuing work to heal any pattern of wounding or trauma. The pattern comes from a traumatic childhood. Also, past lives may be involved.

Talk to a friend or therapist specializing in inner child work, journaling, etc.

"How To Heal the Wound That You've Been Carrying All Your Lives In This Toxic Culture," by Gabor Mate on YouTube.

Gain insight and heal your inner child.

10 - How Can Angels Best Help Healing Inner Child Trauma?

Peace be with you, precious child. Angels hover all about you; They protect you night and day. Angels hover all about you; They will guide you on your way. Songs for the Inner Child by Shaina Noll

My Shadow, like my crippled child, never knew love. In the soul retrieval, it struggled and fought back against the Angels.

When I taught Energy Healing, I would tell the students they could call on Angels for healing. "Angels Please Heal." Light a candle if you like.

About seven in ten U.S. adults say they believe in angels, according to a new poll in 2023.

How Can Angels Heal Your Inner Child?

Call on the Angels: "Angels, Please Help or Heal." You ask for yourself, your inner child, or others. You have to call the Angels.

Calling on Angels can assist in healing your inner child. Your child wants to feel loved, protected, and nurtured.

Call on Angels in Many Different Ways

1. Sit in quiet meditation. Call on Michael, Raphael, Uriel, etc. If you need help, call on a specific situation. Open to hear, feel, or see the Angel.

2. Call in Angels before you go to sleep. You may have a dream. Insights may come the next day.

3. Have a friend assist in a guided meditation. My wife, Lyn, guided me in the meditation below.

Angel Healing for Your Inner Child Trauma

1. See your inner child in the past. Invoke the Angels and ask, "Angels please heal the core trauma of my wounded inner child now." Call upon the Angels now to radiate Divine Love towards the child.

2. See the Golden Light of the Angels embracing your child.

3. Feel and see that light entering and healing the child's physical body, emotions, and mind.

4. Hold an aura of peace and calm from your heart for your child.

5. Observe the event of the trauma as you hold steady, sending love and strength to your child.

6. Allow the Angel's Light and Love through you to your inner child.

7. Now, walk hand in hand with the Angels into and through your child.
8. Come out the other side.
9. Turn around and be in the present time.
10. Leave the entire past trauma behind you, the adult, and your child.

What is Soul Retrieval?

In Angel Healing, you may experience a soul split. This occurs when a part of you or your child splits off because of trauma.

In my soul retrieval, my child struggled and fought back against the Angels. My inner child likes to resist. He wants to be in control—this is his nature. With the Angels, he finally surrendered to Divine peace.

We, as adults, have survived our childhood traumas. Yet, we still suffer from various soul splits due to these traumas. These need soul retrieval.

I have experienced this with clients. When healing occurs, the split-off part returns on its own.

As an adult, you can travel back in time and reconnect with aspects of your inner child. The child split off from its core self as a result of trauma. You have the strength to help your wounded child heal.

On the other hand, Shamanic Healers perform soul retrieval as a service. The shamans recover your vital life force, lost or stolen. You may have a physical or emotional illness as a result. Your integration after the retrieval may take time.

"It has always been the role of the shaman to go into an altered state of consciousness. Track down where the soul fled to in the alternate realities and return it to the client's body." ~ Sandra Ingerman, author of *Soul Retrieval: Mending the Fragmented Self*

Alyson's Healing Journey

Alyson has been involved in her own healing for decades. She also assists others in their healing. May it help you on the path of healing your inner child and trauma.

Alyson describes a challenge as follows: "My path became painful when I took a misstep. I wanted to be like someone I admired. As a result, I ignored my uniqueness."

I knew Alyson when she was a therapist at a group home for teen girls.

Alyson replies, "I did group, family, and individual therapy at the group home. The girls dealt with codependence, individuation, and substance abuse, among other issues. I loved my work. Trauma and attachment disorders were my specialty using EMDR and CBT. I left after eight years to work in California."

EMDR's goal is to help you heal from trauma and distress. The method involves moving your eyes a specific way. This processes traumatic memories.

CBT treatment involves changing thinking patterns—an effective means of treatment for substance abuse.

10 – How Can Angels Best Help Healing Inner Child Trauma

Alyson also calls on Angels and Archangels to heal trauma.

Divine Light Meditation

1. Reaching high above you, connect with the Source of Divine Light, which you will find there.

2. Allow a stream of that Light to flow down, all around you and within you, filling all your cells and atoms with Light.

3. When you are filled to overflowing, allow the Light to flow down through the soles of your feet, deep into the Earth. It connects with the Heart of the Earth Mother, a place of Love and Joy.

4. The Light mixes with this Earth Mother Love energy, blending into a stream of silver and gold sparkling Light.

5. The Light bounces back up as if off a trampoline. This energy blends in, flowing up, filling your body (including arms and hands) up to your heart.

6. From your spiritual heart center, the Light overflows you and expands outward in a blossoming of Light all around you, like you've become a miniature sun.

7. Let this ball of Light keep expanding outward: bigger than the room, bigger than the building, your city, your country, and even bigger than the Earth.

8. Maintain this expansion during the process, returning to refresh and re-expand the Light if necessary.

Alyson describes healing with Archangel Raphael.

Dealing with Archangel Raphael Invocation

Invoke Archangel Raphael by saying: Beloved Archangel Raphael, I ask to do a healing with you.

Name the specific problem (e.g., "Please heal my backache." He has realigned my back.). Archangel Raphael prefers one problem area and to be specific.

Steps

I am healing with Archangel Raphael.

Ask Archangel Raphael

- I connect with the Overnighting Deva of Healing. Wait 15 seconds.
- I connect with Pan. Wait 15 seconds.
- I connect with Archangel Raphael for healing. Wait 15 seconds.
- I connect with my Higher Self. Wait 15 seconds.

During the Healing

You may talk to Archangel Raphael about the issue if you like or not. Set a timer for 10 minutes.

Closing

- Thank Archangel Raphael for the healing.
- Thank each member as you disconnect from them.
- Disconnect from your Higher Self. Wait 15 seconds.

- Disconnect from Archangel Raphael in this coming. Wait 15 seconds.
- Disconnect from Pan. Wait 15 seconds.
- Disconnect from the Overnighting Deva of Healing. Wait 15 seconds.

Resources:

Songs for the Inner Child by Shaina Noll.

"EMDR Therapy: Demonstration and Step-by-Step Walk-through," on YouTube.

"CBT Therapy: Cognitive Behavioral Therapy Exercises (Feel Better!)," on YouTube.

11 - Emotion Code: How to Best Heal Your Heart-Wall

Trapped emotions can create a wall around your heart. This can block you from living life to the fullest. ~ Dr. Bradley Nelson, author of *Emotion Code*

Heart-Walls

What Is the Heart-Wall?

Have you ever felt "heartache" in your life? You may have sensed discomfort in your chest. You suffered deep grief from a loss.

Your subconscious mind forms an energy wall, the "Heart-Wall," which protects your heart from further pain. However, this wall of energy only provides temporary protection.

When you experience further pain, the process repeats itself. This causes your heart wall to grow.

Michael: *I numbed myself to emotions, which are a part of my life. My heart wall protected me from pain, but it also prevented me from feeling connection, joy, and love.*

Heart-walls can form in the womb, at birth, and in childhood. They continue during adolescence and into adulthood. You may experience them in relationships with family, friends, and partners.

These walls trap emotions that remain stuck in your body. This causes energy blocks and pain.

Bradley Nelson's Wife's Heart-Wall Story

Bradley: *My wife's father was a "rage-alcoholic." By age two, her subconscious mind had put up a "wall" around her little heart to protect it. Over the years, we surmised that extra layers were added to this Heart-Wall.*

As she grew up, my wife always felt a bit numb to emotions. She always wondered why she couldn't feel things as deeply as others. When with friends, she never felt like she belonged. She always felt as if she were on the outside looking in.

After the last Trapped Emotion released from her Heart-Wall, she felt she belonged. Emotions took on a new richness. She was able to feel on a new level."

Emotion Code

The Emotion Code is an energy healing technique that helps identify and release trapped emotions that result from negative past events or trauma.

Trapped emotions may cause depression and anxiety. They can block you from love and happiness. You may feel disconnected from others.

Michael: *Years ago, I studied and used the* Emotion Code *by Dr. Bradley Nelson.*

Removing Heart-Walls with the Emotion Code Book

The Emotion Code works with your subconscious mind and body. It uses muscle testing to identify your trapped emotions. Then, release can occur.

Your trapped emotions create physical and psychological issues. These patterns stem from childhood and other traumatic events.

Your negative experiences and unresolved emotional conflicts (Shadows) also contribute. Your body's energy flow becomes disrupted. You feel discomfort or even illness.

Benefits of Removing Your Heart-Walls

Releasing trapped emotions leads to profound shifts in your consciousness. True healing requires addressing the root cause of disease.

Benefits can include better energy and healthier relationships. You realize more abundance and a greater sense of purpose, leading to greater happiness and well-being.

According to Bradley Nelson, most people tend to have between 15 and 30 Heart-Wall emotions, which can be higher or lower.

Are you ready to heal the pain of your heart wall?

My Heart-Wall Inner Child Healing - Alina MaChita

"The Emotion Code healing process can finally uncover these 'Inner Child' trapped emotions. They release during several sessions. Otherwise, you will continue to create the same life drama repeatedly. Many people live their existing life in a grown-up's body but with a child's mind.

"As an adult, your inner child yearns for attention and support. Change and release your inner child's story." ~ Alina MaChita, Executive Contributor, Brainz Magazine

The following details an example of my Heart-Wall healing. In the healing, I intuitively sensed the Angels as they assisted. Archangel Michael also works closely with me daily as a guide.

The Emotion Code uses no Angels. You can read the book and do your own session, as described in the book. You can also contact an Emotion Code therapist.

I had the help of a professional Energy Healer, Lyn, and Angels to guide me. Lyn has the gift of holding a safe container for clients. She feels and sees energetically what occurs for the client. The child referred to is my inner child.

The inner child contained all my positive and negative emotional patterns from childhood. It lived in my body and subconscious.

Lyn: *Michael, let the Angels help you.*

Michael: *I feel agitation. I sense my Shadow resisting the healing. I want to escape feeling stuck.*

Lyn: *Michael, keep staying with the energy and your feelings.*

Michael: *That damned Shadow. Then I remembered, "The only way out is through."*

Lyn: *Be aware. Avoid getting caught in judgment. Your Shadow, like a neglected child, hides stuck in darkness. It never knew what it was like to be in the Light. It lives in a "Garden of Death" where no life exists.*

Michael: As the healing proceeded, I experienced sadness and pain in all areas of my body. Then I sensed my Shadow disappearing. The Angels told me to reconnect.

Lyn: *Your Shadow is your dark side. It is in your subconscious. Your Shadow within you feels scared, ashamed, and unworthy.*

Michael, connect your heart and inner child to the Shadow—all parts in all times and dimensions. Feel and contain all the sadness and agony of your inner child. Then, a healing ground or womb can form. Quiet your mind. Allow your child to go deeper into the past (past lives).

In the past, you have given your energies and power away to everyone else. Now, invite your inner child to receive the healing. Breathe in the Angels' sweetness into your lungs.

Divine Grace comes in as the pain and the old leave. Your heart-wall dissolves. The Light and darkness of the Shadow begin to flow into one another.

Michael: *I feel the flow.*

Lyn: *The more you surrender to Divine Grace, the more the Light moves into the Shadow. The Shadow and pain dissolve into the Light. Your body will relax. You may feel peace at some point.*

Michael: *Yes, I feel my whole-body relaxing.*

Lyn: *Beautiful. Your structure of pain, the heart-wall, is dissolving.*

Michael: *A tear trickled down my right cheek. I realized I had been stuck at the age of a five-year-old boy.*

This boy had buried his feelings and trauma. He stayed invisible in the family to survive.

I sensed my inner child coming back home to me.

I thanked the Angels and Lyn with gratitude. Thank You, Thank You, Thank You. **Session Ended.**

Your patterns stem from childhood trauma and other events. It takes ongoing sessions to continue to heal.

Unless you allow healing to occur, the emotional pain will increase. Do you leave your child by themselves to "tough it out?" Pain needs loving. A child in pain needs loving.

Your inner child may fight against healing with its personal will, and Divine Grace will not be able to enter for healing.

Your thinking is part of the fight. When your mind chatters, no space exists for Divine Grace. Learning to still your mind creates room for Divine Grace.

Bradley Nelson Testimonials:

Bradley Nelson's "Do-You-Have-a-Heart-Wall" website has two testimonials. These are of people's heart-walls he has cleared.

First Testimonial Bradley's female client, *So, for all of you who think women cannot marry after a certain age, get your Heart-Wall cleared. Stay open to the possibilities life has to offer. Remember my story. We are now approaching our fifth anniversary.*

Second Testimonial Bradley, *One-by-one, we cleared each of these emotions. In the end, I asked her body if the Heart-Wall had finally been released. Her body said that it was completely gone.*

Removing Heart-Walls with the Emotion Code Book

1. **Understanding and Identifying Emotions.** One of the key lessons in The Emotion Code is learning to understand and identify different emotions. The book teaches techniques to help you recognize and acknowledge your emotions.

2. **Emotional Trapped Energies.** The Emotion Code introduces the concept of trapped emotions. These emotions can get lodged in the body and cause physical and emotional imbalances. The book teaches methods to release these trapped energies.

3. **Muscle Testing.** The Emotion Code explains the technique of muscle testing. This identifies trapped emotions in the body. This technique involves applying gentle pressure to specific muscles. The body's response determines the presence of trapped emotions.

4. **Releasing Trapped Emotions.** The book provides step-by-step instructions on how to release trapped

emotions. It uses a technique called the "Emotion Code Chart." This chart helps you identify the specific emotion, allowing steps to be released through techniques such as magnet therapy or deep breathing exercises.

5. **Healing and Self-Care.** The Emotion Code emphasizes the importance of self-care and emotional healing. Focus on emotional healing as an integral part of your health journey.

Dr. Bradly Nelson States:

I believe that the single most important thing you can do for yourself is to get rid of the trapped negative emotions forming a wall around your heart.

The Emotion Code® is the only way I know to do this. Anyone can easily learn it, and no previous training is required.

I believe the release of Trapped Emotions is permanent. It works for all ages.

By helping people shed their emotional baggage, we can help them obtain the potential to become empowered.

Resources:

The Emotion Code: How to Release Your Trapped Emotions for Abundant Health, Love, and Happiness, by Dr. Bradley Nelson.

"Emotion Code" by Dr. Bradley Nelson. He walks you through the process of releasing your first trapped emotion, on YouTube.

"What Is the Heart-Wall: Origin Story" with Dr. Bradley Nelson and Jean Nelson, on YouTube.

12 - How to Overcome Drama Triangle of Relationship Victim, Rescuer, Abuser Conflict

> *The Victim is not really as helpless as they feel. The Rescuer doesn't really help, and the Persecutor doesn't really have a valid claim.* ~ Stephen Karpman, author of *Drama Triangle*

Drama Triangle

Karpman placed these three roles in an inverted triangle.

The three roles in the victim triangle are Victim, Rescuer, and Persecutor/Abuser.

He described them as being the three faces of the victim.

- On the top of the triangle rests Victim - Poor Me.
- The left side is Rescuer - Let Me Help You.
- On the right side is Abuser - It's All Your Fault.

Karpman, a psychiatrist, presented the Drama Triangle in 1968. It maps out destructive interaction among people in conflict. The triangle of actors is persecutors, victims, and rescuers. It is used as a tool in psychotherapy.

Empaths and extra sensitives to find this information useful. Parents with sensitive children and regular people can benefit from understanding and overcoming relationship conflict.

What Role Do You Play the Most?
1. Victim - This is when you feel like a victim. Your stance is "Poor Me." You may feel ashamed or powerless. Do you remain in a relationship with an abuser? Are you creating rescuers in your life? Do you ignore your feelings or avoid change?
2. Rescuer - Rescuer always wants to help others. Do you avoid your problems?
3. Abuser – Do you blame others? It's all their fault. Do you become defensive if blamed?

Until you become aware of your role, you cannot transform.

Relationship Conflict Persecutor/Abuser
1. Abusers act as blamers, bullies, controllers, and critics. It's all your fault!
2. Abusers need scapegoats.
3. Abusers criticize and get angry. They can be over-critical parents.
4. Sometimes, they're narcissists. They focus only on getting their needs met. I know many of the client's parents like this.

I picked up my father's abusive anger toward my mother. For years, I felt anger at my mother for no reason.

Victim-Rescuer-Abuser Roles I Learned in My Family

I learned roles passed on down from our father and mother's lineages, roles in which my DNA carried a tendency of victim-rescuer-abuser.

Abuser: The Bully–As an Abuser, my father never attempted to overcome his powerlessness and shame. He became belligerent with his drinking buddies in town. For twenty years, he bullied and emotionally and verbally abused my mother. He denied his inadequacies by victimizing my mother. So, I know he felt like a Victim. He did express Victim in that the world owed him a living.

Rescuer: As a young girl, my mother became a caretaker/rescuer of five other children. Her mother had died young. She lived on a farm with lots of back-breaking work from dawn to dusk. In our family, my mother took on the victim/martyr role. As a teen, she once told me, "Look at all I've sacrificed for you kids."

I learned unconsciously to take on a parental role from a young age. Without knowing it, I filled in for my father. I learned to be a victim.

As a young boy, I made unconscious decisions to feel somewhat safe. I stayed quiet, expressed nothing, and repressed my feelings. Anger, I repressed at the deepest levels.

For survival, I allowed myself to be a victim of my father's anger. I decided it was unsafe to express anger. As a result,

I carried many layers of anger throughout my life. Only extreme provocation evoked a state of rage.

Overcoming Relationship Conflict Victim Abuser from Others

In my thirties, I had four major relationships with women. They lasted about three years each. In three relationships, I existed in a state of numbness. I feared being vulnerable and expressing feelings. As a result, I took on the Victim role. My partners fell into Abusers/Critics blaming me for my lack of expression. In truth, these women had little skill in being vulnerable. They seldom expressed their feelings aside from frustration and anger. We were two peas in a pod, swimming in suffering.

In my second relationship, a few months of hypnosis gave me strength and courage. I then requested the woman to move out. I had provided for all her living needs for three years.

In the third relationship, I keep being the Rescuer. I wanted the woman to become healthier physically. She had experienced the victimization of severe physical abuse from her previous husband.

She introduced me to the concept of codependency recovery and inner child healing. This benefited me greatly.

I fell into the fourth relationship with no physical attraction whatsoever. We had a common service goal of creating a healing institute.

12 – How to Overcome Drama Triangle of Relationship Victim, Rescuer, Abuser Conflict

This woman had been severely mistreated by a narcissistic mother. On the outside, she presented as a successful career woman. On the inside, she had extremely fragile self-esteem. As an Abuser, she blamed and criticized me a lot.

My Recovery

- I learned to begin to say "No."
- I set healthy boundaries.
- I began to know my needs.
- I started nurturing myself.

Overcoming Relationship Conflict Victim Abuser

- Abusers can learn and change unconscious acts to conscious ones.
- Can become more flexible.
- Learn to feel vulnerable.
- Assist in problem-solving with others.
- It also explains how to help us understand our dysfunctional behavioral patterns.

How My Wife and I Overcame Drama Triangle of Relationship Conflict

Like me, my wife of thirty years came from a family of five. She suffered as a Victim of her mother's alcoholism. As the eldest, she took on the role of mother of the family. She protected her siblings, the best she could, from her mother's behaviors.

In my wife's role as a Rescuer, she developed extreme codependency. When she visited her mother, she set strong personal boundaries as an adult. If her mother had been drinking, she left. She no longer accepted victimization. So, she graduated from Victim to Teacher.

When we met, I had spent half my life on a path of emotional and spiritual growth. My wife had been a party girl seeking outer pleasures. She zoomed ahead of me when she embraced an inner path of growth.

My wife studied some healing courses and attended the Oneness University in India courses five times over a period of years.

As a result, she connected with her Inner Divine. Her Divine guided her in overcoming being a Rescuer and a Codependent.

One day, after some years, my wife told me, she would no longer be my emotional body. I had to be in touch with my feelings and express them.

Personal Responsibility and Self-Empowerment

My wife and I graduated from our family patterns of Victim and Rescuer. We now work as a duo of energetic healers and teachers. Clients experience emotional and spiritual life transformations.

12 – How to Overcome Drama Triangle of Relationship Victim, Rescuer, Abuser Conflict

We have developed our professional gifts as Energy Healers and Spiritual Teachers. We have refined our empathic sensitivity to subtle energies. We also experience humanity's collective energies.

At some point, your consciousness starts to shift. You move out of your personal self to feeling world group consciousness. This world consciousness contains all the hatred in the world. It also includes all the loving acts for the betterment of humanity.

My wife reciprocates with her gifts to assist me emotionally in my healing. I assist her physical and energetic being. She no longer gets caught in her critical mind or emotional drama.

My inner child sometimes still falls into the Victim pit of Poor Me. My wife lovingly points this out to me. "Michael, you have fallen into the pit again."

I have learned what it feels like in the emotional swamp of the pit. By intent to raise my consciousness, I come out.

Further, my inner child still wants recognition for doing a good job. When I see this, I inwardly gather him up in my arms. Then, I connect both of us with our Divine Essence, where we just Be.

I also still wrestle sometimes with wanting to fix and save people.

With more consciousness, I have a choice for responsibility and greater self-empowerment. I can continue with old patterns that keep me locked into suffering or choose a new paradigm of evolving beyond suffering—a paradigm of joy in Life.

The Following is a Client's Experience as a Victim, Rescuer, and Abuser

Melinda has received hundreds of hours of training, including yoga, meditation, counseling, and energy work. Most of her training is self-healing.

My wife, Lyn, and I assist in a phone session. We both hold a safe, sacred space for the client. Lyn has the intuitive ability to see and feel. She uses this to connect and guide the client.

Melinda: *In my session with Lyn and Michael, I talked about doubting myself. Also, I dislike working with male teachers. This occurs when we do group work together in a class.*

Lyn: *Melinda, doubting yourself is an aspect of being a victim. You also give away your power. Michael and I will energetically clear you of your past working with male teachers.*

Michael and Lyn use intent to clear Melinda. Michael plays a crystal bowl. Lyn strikes a tuning fork.

Lyn: *Melinda, your fear draws men to you who want to crush the life out of you. These men sense your vulnerability. They enjoy abusing and bullying you. Control makes them feel powerful.*

Melinda: *My husband always wants to be in control also.*

Lyn: *Melinda, breathe. Face your inner fear. Breathe through your body. You hold doubt in your belly.*

Melinda: *I have thoughts that I am not good enough.*

Lyn: *The energy of the earth is coming up your feet now. Breathe it into your belly and that part that never feels good enough. The energy strengthens your emotional heart. Melinda, I see you once had a connection with Joan of Arc. She was a warrioress for the*

French and followed her inner visions. I see your Divine Presence coming through your body.

Melinda: *I feel a fortitude, a strength now.*

Lyn: *Congratulations. Your homework is to breathe in your divine presence daily.* **Session Ended.**

For more help, find a coach or therapist. Someone who specializes in codependence recovery, trauma, or victim consciousness.

"Understanding Codependency and the Drama Trauma Triangle," on YouTube.

Codependent No More, by Melody Beattie, 2nd Edition.

13 - How to Overcome Drama Triangle of Relationship Victim Conflict

What you think, you become. What you feel, you attract. ~ Buddha

The energy/frequency we put out through our thoughts and emotions mirrors back to us. Our relationships reflect what we think and feel within ourselves. Many times, these inner sensations may be unconscious.

Do you know you have the power to change your inner reality? This then changes what occurs around you.

You may react with anger, avoidance, or blame the other person. You may see yourself as a victim. Then fear, anger, illness, or suffering results.

How Does Victim Mentality Affect Relationships?

The victim mentality can hinder open and effective communication. The focus is often on blame and self-pity. You could have a productive dialogue. Instead, one partner takes on the role of the victim. Meanwhile, the other feels burdened or overwhelmed.

Three Methods for Dissolving Victim Patterns

1. Journaling

Draw the drama triangle diagram.

Write down the victim, rescuer, or abuser relationships you experience most for yourself.

Write down the victim, rescuer, or abuser relationships you experience most with others.

2. How to Dissolve Your Victim Patterns with Self-Help Focusing

You may find that focusing also works for dissolving Rescuer and Abuser patterns.

Psychotherapist Eugene Gendlin developed Focusing in the 1960s. You can learn to use it for your therapy or adapt it to become more aware of your victim/shadow patterns.

Focusing involves holding attention to sensations in your body. Breathe into the sensation. Be open and nonjudgemental. Keep coming back to the sensation when your mind wanders. Pay attention to your intuitive knowing, images, or intuitive sensing.

Develop the ability to spend fifteen to twenty minutes at a time. Like any skill, focus takes time to develop. Learning a meditation practice helps. Practice meditation daily.

3. Gendlin's Six-Step Focusing Meditative Self-Help Process

1. **Clearing a Space:** Let go of all outside cares. Create a quiet place inside yourself. Breathe. Notice the tension and release it with your breath.

2. **Getting a Felt Sense:** Ask an open-ended question. How does this victim/shadow pattern feel inside my body? Where do I feel it the most? Do not analyze your mind. Wait until you get an intuitive or body sense.

3. **Finding a Handle:** Wait until you get words, a sensation, or an image. Your sense may be vague at first.

4. **Resonating and Checking:** Take the word(s), sensation, or image and ask, "Is this it?" Keep sensing and checking until you know, see, or feel it is the right "fit."

5. **Asking:** If necessary, keep asking open-ended questions. Return to steps two, three, and four until there is a right "fit." You may feel a temporary increase in tension, or on the other hand, there may be a release of tension. Insight or emotions may arise.

6. **Receiving:** Throughout, breathe deep into your belly. Breath creates space for Divine Grace and intuitive solutions—solutions beyond your thinking mind.

Keep practicing Focusing until the victim/shadow pattern eventually dissolves. It will probably be gradual. Notice the small steps with gratitude.

Focusing-Oriented Psychotherapy: A Manual of the Experiential Method by Eugene Gendlin.

Third Method for Dissolving Victim Patterns

You have sixty-four DNA codes. Within your unconscious and body, you have victim patterns. Eleven out of sixty-four possible shadow frequencies relate to you. These mental and emotional patterns arise out of your anger and fears. You express and encounter them through personal drama and relationship conflicts.

Richard Rudd's book *The Gene Keys* explains the sixty-four victim/shadow patterns. You can receive a free profile identifying your specific eleven shadow patterns. You will also receive an introduction to reading your profile. Go to Gene Keys Free Profile on Rudd's website. See *The Gene Keys* book on Amazon.

When you accept and begin dissolving your shadows, your suffering lessens. Also, your gifts and siddhis (flowering of gifts) start emerging.

"Embrace the Shadow, Release the Gift, Embody the Siddhi."
~ Richard Rudd

You feel the effect of collective humanity's fears. You also experience some aspects of humanity's sixty-four shadows/victim patterns.

How to Dissolve Your DNA Victim Patterns with the Gene Keys

Deprogram your DNA with lower-frequency patterns of victim/shadow. Eventually, reprogram with the higher frequencies of your gifts and siddhi's.

Victim patterns dissolve using three tools. Use these tools to take action: Awareness, Compassion, and Transmutation (ACT).

Journal – Write your impressions in a notebook

1. Awareness

- Notice when you fall into victim. (Recall the details).
- What event occurred? (i.e., disagreement with a partner).
- What did you feel? (i.e., anger or loss of energy).
- What thoughts did you have? (i.e., I am never listened to, or I better just be quiet).

2. Compassion

- Be patient with yourself. (It takes ongoing effort over time).
- Accept and embrace your shadow like it's a small child.
- See how your victim no longer serves you.
- Notice the repeating emotions and beliefs that give the victim/shadow life.

3. Transformation

- Call in the Divine Light/Higher Power or the Gift related to the victim/shadow.
- Notice where you feel the shadow sensations in your body.
- Focus your attention and keep breathing into that area, i.e., your belly.
- Stay focused and breathing until you notice some change.

Repeat the tool that works for you each time the victim/shadow appears. With intent, Divine Light begins to dissolve your shadows.

The Following is a Client's Experience. It shows how being a Victim creates conflict in relationships.

Lina is an Energy Healer who offers Body Work and Shamanic Energy Healing. For a decade, she has helped clients release stress and trauma and experience wellness.

My wife, Lyn, and I assisted in a phone session. We both held a safe, sacred space for the client. Lyn has the intuitive ability to see and feel. She uses this to connect with and guide the client.

Lina: *In my session with Lyn and Michael, I talked about how, growing up, I experienced constant doubt. As a young girl, I acted like a tomboy. I spent my time outside climbing trees and in nature by myself.*

My mother showed no affection to me. She never received love from her parents. I never even received hugs from her.

My father also ignored me. He refused to call me by my name.

As an adult, my mother married a completely self-absorbed man.

You can see the pattern. I had little sense of self-worth. Most of the time, I felt an emptiness and a lack of connection with people.

Lyn: *Lina, your inner child wants control. She's afraid of never being seen. You have a choice. Choose life. I see you going through a big shift in your life. Your child wants to distract you. She wants to imbalance you. Breathe in Divine Grace.*

Lina: *What is Grace?*

Lyn: *Good question. I sense your body has never known Grace.*

I have a quote from Yogananda. He was an East Indian who taught Kriya yoga meditation in the U.S.

"God's grace flows into us the more we open ourselves to Him. It doesn't come to us from outside. It is the operation, from within, of our own higher reality. Grace comes the more we live in soul-consciousness, the less we live centered in the ego."

Lina: *I feel more centered and aligned in my body.*

Lyn: *Lina, you have allowed the Grace to begin entering your body. Practice centering daily and breathing the Grace in.* **Session Ended.**

Lina's childhood trauma of little parental love left her doubting her worth. She never directly fell into the victim role of "Poor Me." Yet she felt alone, vulnerable, and unsafe. As a result, she tended to control the expression of her feelings.

Lina's doubt and lack of belief in herself are aspects of a victim.

It is possible to break free of being a victim.

Resources:

Open to learning to feel inner feelings and express them. Find a therapist who works with childhood trauma.

Take a course in positive communication skills.

Learn a meditation method to focus your mind.

Join a codependency recovery group.

Read *Focusing-Oriented Psychotherapy* by Eugene Gendlin.

14 - Subpersonalities: How to Better Recognize and Transform Them

Conflicting internal voices are normal. Instead of being only one person, we all hold subpersonalities within ourselves. They relate to each other in the same ways that members of a family might relate to one another. ~ Richard C. Schwartz, Psychotherapist, author of *You Are the One You've Been Waiting For*

What Are Subpersonalities?

Have you ever felt a childlike vulnerability or experienced a critical voice inside you? This voice dominated your consciousness. Welcome to some of your subpersonalities.

Many different selves/subpersonalities live within each of you. Each has its feelings and thoughts. They form at different ages due to life experiences to protect you.

Knowing and embracing your subpersonalities, you develop more compassion. You accept your relationship with yourself. This leads to greater self-awareness and personal growth.

Common Subpersonalities

- Inner Critic.
- Perfectionist.
- People-Pleaser.
- Rebel.
- Inner Child., etc.

Inner Family Subpersonalities (These represent the four directions).

- Inner Nurturer.
- Inner Child.
- Inner Sage.
- Inner Warrior.

Subpersonalities represent many aspects of your personality, including all the different types of people inside you. These aspects influence how you perceive your world. The inner family manifests in your outer relationships. When balanced and healthy, you have successful relationships.

How to Recognize Your Subpersonalities

- Have you ever felt there is more than one you?
- Are you sometimes one type of person and sometimes another?
- Do you ever say "YES" when you meant to say "NO"?
- Do you decide to do one thing, then do something else?

14 – Subpersonalities: How to Better Recognize and Transform Them

Discovering and Transforming Your Subpersonalities

"Subpersonalities reside as thoughts, feelings, and sensations in your body. These act like another person for you to cope with. Many times, they developed because of childhood trauma." ~ John Rowan

John Rowan Discover Your Subpersonalities: Our Inner World and the People in It.

John Rowan, Author, and Psychologist, answers questions about subpersonalities. There are exercises and questionnaires. The processes enable you to take charge of your subpersonalities.

Transforming Shadow Subpersonalities

"When you accept and begin dissolving your shadows, your suffering lessens. Also, your gifts and siddhis (flowering of gifts) start emerging. Embrace the Shadow, Release the Gift, Embody the Siddhi." ~ Richard Rudd, author of *The Gene Keys*

There are sixty-four Shadow Subpersonalities. Eleven out of sixty-four shadow frequencies relate to you. These mental and emotional patterns arise out of your anger and fears. You encounter them through personal drama and relationship conflicts.

Richard Rudd, in his book *The Gene Keys*, explains the sixty-four victim/shadow patterns. On Rudd's website, you can receive a free profile identifying your eleven shadow patterns.

You will also receive an intro on how to begin to read your profile.

Go to Gene Keys Free Profile on Rudd's website. Gene Keys.com.

See *The Gene Keys: Embracing Your Higher Purpose*, on Amazon.

Roberto Assagioli Transforming Consciousness

"We identify with the roles we play in life. With the masks within us and with our idols. It is a 'release,' a liberation and awakening of hidden potential." ~ Roberto Assagioli, author of *Transpersonal Development: The Dimension Beyond Psychosynthesis*

Psychosynthesis is a practical therapy designed to help people achieve their full potential. It evolved out of fifty years of Assagioli's psychospiritual reflections.

Part One describes the reality of the superconscious. Part Two delves into the problems and difficulties experienced on the spiritual path. Part three deals with the everyday application of those insights.

Dan Millman, author of *Way of the Peaceful Warrior*

"In my youth, I focused on self-improvement. Then, one day, I realized that no matter how much I improved myself, only one person benefited. If I could influence other people in a positive way, that made my life more meaningful and exciting." ~ Dan Millman *Way of the Peaceful Warrior*

The subpersonalities of the inner family include the Inner Nurturer, Inner Child, Inner Sage, and Inner Warrior. Millman describes in his book the functional aspect of the inner warrior.

14 – Subpersonalities: How to Better Recognize and Transform Them

Quotes from *Way of the Peaceful Warrior*, by Dan Millman

- A warrior does not give up what he loves, and he finds the love in what he does.
- The journey is what brings us happiness, not the destination.
- You cannot attain happiness; it attains you - only after you surrender everything else.
- The secret of happiness, you see, is not found in seeking more, but in developing the capacity to enjoy less.
- Everything you'll ever need to know is within you; the secrets of the universe are imprinted on the cells of your body.

In *Way of the Peaceful Warrior,* the old man arouses Millman's curiosity. He learns the path of the peaceful warrior, a life philosophy that teaches how to live with focus and intention. You learn to transform passive feelings like sadness or fear into positive action.

- Millman describes the laws of proper relationships.
- Exchanging things with others for mutual benefit.
- Creating harmony and balance in your life.
- Cultivating gentleness and gratitude.
- Sacrificing yourself for the greater good.
- Maintaining healthy boundaries. This is your warrior armor.

Almine Your Subpersonalities: The Key to Successful Relationships

"The subpersonalities of the psyche represent the directions, a navigational system with which we decide which qualities of a specific direction we wish to emphasize in the expressions of our lives. The subpersonalities of the Inner Nurturer, Inner Child, Inner Sage, and Inner Warrior (the four directions) are used to relate in physical life." ~ The Seer Almine

Almine talks about the functional and dysfunctional aspects of these subpersonalities. The subpersonalities in the Medicine Wheel embody the Four Directions. The Medicine Wheel manifests as Father Sky, Mother Earth, and Spirit. These all represent aspects of health and the cycles of life.

In personal inner journeys for clients, I take them to physical Medicine Wheels. Then, we explore how the four subpersonalities show up in their daily lives.

Dysfunctional Inner Nurturer

A critical parent represents a dysfunctional nurturer. They judge what a child does and how the child does it. Examples of dysfunctional nurturers include the addict, codependent, and people pleaser or rescuer. More examples include authoritarian, perfectionistic, punishing, or withdrawn fathers or mothers.

Functional Inner Nurturer

In the Medicine Wheel, the inner nurturer resides in the South. This is the loving mother. She provides food, love, and safety for the child's growth. She allows the inner child to have a voice. She encourages healthy self-expression. She gives the inner child time to play. This is also the loving father.

Dysfunctional Inner Child

A dysfunctional inner child wants to be in control. This occurs out of fear and when healthy needs are ignored. The unhealthy inner child lacks self-esteem. The unhealthy inner child says, "I feel less than; look at me; I need; I want." Do you allow your inner child to run your life? Does your inner child feel abandoned?

Functional Inner Child

In the Medicine Wheel, the inner child resides in the West. This child is about five years old.

It needs to be nurtured and properly parented. Allow the child to express themselves in healthy ways. Set healthy boundaries. Engage in play and enjoyable activities.

Dysfunctional Inner Sage

A dysfunctional sage judges you for your beliefs. This results when you have different views or lifestyles. The sage looks for truth outside of self. The sage judges a situation or person rather than using the gift of discernment.

When dysfunctional, subpersonalities neglect their roles. As a result, the Inner Child may show up at inappropriate times. This is because it lacks nurturing and feels unsafe and unwanted.

Functional Inner Sage

The inner sage/wise woman resides in the East. They have intuition and inner wisdom. They commune with the Divine within. They look for anything left in the deeper layers of the subconscious that still needs healing. They use discernment to offer direction to others. Wise counsel comes from them.

Dysfunctional Inner Warrior

A dysfunctional warrior fights against external circumstances. They want to oppose and smash. No protection or boundaries assist other inner family members. They strengthen that which they oppose. They indulge in limited thinking and cannot protect the inner child's innocence. The warrior also protects the inner sage's sacredness and the inner nurturer's gentleness. They also have activities that replenish. They live passionately. They work and play awareness of what they like or need to nourish their strength.

Functional Inner Warrior

The inner warrior/warrioress resides in the North. They guide and guard the inner family setting safe boundaries are set up to protect the innocence of the inner child. The warrior also protects the sacredness of the inner sage and the gentleness of the inner nurturer. They also have activities that replenish them. They live passionately. They work and play at what makes the heart sing.

Examine and make notes where you are functional or dysfunctional in your daily life.

How to Discover the Subpersonalities Running Your Life?

I had yet to learn of the nature of subpersonalities.

My father, an alcoholic, passed away some thirty-five years ago. He had lived in great, unexpressed emotional pain. He shut himself off from everyone, including me. I had yearned for my father's presence.

Depression and a feeling of powerlessness had pervaded most of my life. Under the depression lurked the feeling of powerlessness. Also, being a victim, I felt I had no choices beyond my childhood trauma.

For two-thirds of my life, I believed something was inherently wrong with me.

Exploring a Subpersonality

In early 2012, I experienced a healing of a major subpersonality. A gifted, Energetic Healer, Lyn O'Hara, assisted. She facilitated the identification and integration of a subpersonality.

The session begins.

Lyn: *Connect with your Divine/higher/True Self and ask for your Divine Self to come into your body. I sense a subconscious subpersonality in your heart.*

Stay in your Observer Self. Be present as an impartial watcher of what you feel in your body.

Your subpersonality is getting bigger. Now, it is contracting, shrinking, and hiding in a cave.

Michael: *I sense a coldness in my chest. There is a lot of tension. Now, I am feeling abandoned. What is happening?*

Lyn: *An abandoned child believes it did something wrong. Every subpersonality has a thought form attached to it. Michael, what is your thought?*

Michael: *I am waiting for an answer from my intuition. I am not enough/not good enough.*

Lyn: *Continue to hold that thought. Hold it like a baby in your arms. Love it. Keep the perspective of the observer and stay present.'*

I see a man coming in. It is your father. He is asking for forgiveness.

Michael: *I sensed my father standing before me. He is a gentle, sensitive man I had never known. Sadness overwhelmed me, and I offered him forgiveness.*

Lyn: *This experience with your father of abandonment created a rift. A pain that had a part of you split off. It fragmented into a separate subpersonality.*

Good work. Congratulations. Subpersonalities can never be healed through the use of your mind. You will never heal a subpersonality by understanding it or thinking it through. Your mind only creates more separation. **Session Ended.**

Healing Subpersonalities

You need to be familiar with a specific subpersonality to do this process yourself. Otherwise, find a professional to help you.

1. First, the subpersonality needs to be separated from all parts of your body.

2. Second, you heal a subpersonality by calling forth your Divine Self through intent or prayer.
3. Third, be present and experience the sensations of where the subpersonality resides in your body.
4. Fourthly, focus on the Divine spark in your heart.
5. Fifth, breathe into the subpersonality and be with it. Let any thoughts that emerge wanting to interfere fall away.
6. Sixth, you will be tested in your everyday world. When a subpersonality emerges into your awareness, practice steps 1 to 5.

Do You Want to Heal Your Subpersonalities?

- Find an energy healer who has experience with subpersonalities.
- Find a therapist who understands subpersonalities and heals from the heart.

Meditation will assist in identifying subpersonalities. Focus each day on the Divine Spark in your heart chakra, which is in the middle of your chest. Guard your thoughts and feelings. Produce thoughts for the highest possible empowerment.

- Breathe into your heart. Be with the sensations there. Let any thoughts that arise fall away. Come back to the spark in your heart. Do this as often as possible to discover your subpersonalities.

Read *Way of the Peaceful Warrior: A Book That Changes Lives* by Dan Millman.

15 – Codependency:
How to Feel Your Best and Recover

Low self-esteem is rooted in the need to please, people-pleasing, and codependency. Overcome the need to please and feel confident. ~ Sharon Martin, Psychotherapist and Codependency Expert

What is Codependency?

- Focus on other people's problems, feelings, and needs.
- Ignoring your feelings and needs.
- Seeing other people as more important than yourself.
- Taking care of others to feel worthwhile.
- Being overly dependent on others emotionally.

How many of the above behaviors have you experienced? I have encountered most of them.

It's helpful to think of codependency on a spectrum. That is, some people experience more symptoms and distress than others.

Possibly, over 90 percent of the American population demonstrates some form of codependent behavior. This has been my experience with clients.

What is a Codependent Relationship?

- Codependent relationships are unbalanced. Typically, one person becomes overly responsible, enabling the other to underfunction and avoid responsibility.
- You can develop a codependent relationship with a spouse, child, parent, or friend.
- Codependents focus on trying to help and control other people.

What Causes Codependency?

Dysfunctional families struggle with codependency in adulthood. Codependent traits usually develop as a result of childhood trauma. Codependent traits serve a purpose in childhood. They help you cope with unpredictable family lives.

How Do You Recover?

- Make your own needs a priority.
- Know what you need and ask for it.
- Learn healthy communication.
- Stand up for yourself.
- Set boundaries.
- Create relationships where you give and also receive.
- Practice self-compassion.

15 – Codependency: How to Feel Your Best and Recover

Sharon Martin is a licensed psychotherapist and codependency expert. She's the author of *The Better Boundaries Workbook*. In the workbook, follow simple writing prompts. Bolster your communication skills. Learn to establish and maintain better boundaries.

Four Stages of Relationship Development

Dependence to Codependence to Independence to Interdependence

The entire discussion is about how crucial relationships are to your consciousness. The last stage, "Interdependence," allows and celebrates diversity and unity. The Seer Almine explains the Alchemy of Relationships.

1. **Dependence:** In this stage, similarities are stressed. Couples experience this as their initial stage of being "in love." They feel euphoric because they see themselves in the other person's mirror. Culturally, this manifests as tribal life, where the individual is expected to behave in a certain way in exchange for the tribe's support.

2. **Codependence:** Some individuality is expressed. There is still a strong desire to identify with each other. No one steps too far out of "the box." Many tribal members in North America are in this stage. They live in the city and keep strong ties of dependence with the tribe.

3. **Independence:** In personal interaction, each individual becomes almost desperate to find his or her own

identity. Differences are now emphasized. In modern, mechanized societies, all types of assurances are needed. There is no tribal support. In apartments, people live without knowing their neighbor's name.

4. **Interdependence:** If stage 3 survives, this stage brings stability. The individuals are secure in their relationships. They support each other's differences. This is the template for communal living for the future. A group lives together because of a common goal. They are free to express and grow in diversity.

In the stage of unity within diversity, interdependence maximizes chances. Thus, individual growth contributes to the growth of the group.

My Codependency: Difficulty Recognizing and Expressing Feeling

I struggled with codependency into my fifties.

Feelings – I relied on my female partners to feel for me. Rather than knowing and expressing my feelings, I denied my feelings and needs. Growing up and into my thirties, I felt numb. My feelings were frozen. I seldom felt connected to others. Afraid to show my needs, I ignored them. For decades, I denied and avoided facing my inner emotional pain. I trusted no one.

Focused on Others – I attracted girlfriends who needed me to provide a place to live. My self-esteem depended on taking care of whoever was my girlfriend. My boundaries are emotionally entangled with my girlfriend's boundaries. I put others' needs before my own.

Self-Sacrifice – I sacrificed to take care of other people's financial needs. For six months, I assisted in teaching outdoor seminars in different states. I paid $5000 for the main instructor's accommodation and meals. I never depend on anyone. I believe in doing everything myself.

Control – My girlfriend and I each wanted to be in control, which led to many verbal arguments. Lacking control at times, I felt powerless. I had difficulty saying "No." Pushed to the limit by one girlfriend, I exploded in rage. I am a perfectionist. I used to live in my head. I wanted to figure everything out.

Tips for Codependency Recovery

- Become willing to open your mind, expand your perception of yourself, your feelings, and others, and explore the gray areas between black and white.

- Begin to trust yourself. Become aware of what you feel in your body. Your body never lies. Begin to trust your first impressions. Also, trust your heart and your intuition.

- Find a good inner child therapist. They can help you heal your childhood trauma.

- Learn grounding exercises to connect to the earth. Start seeing and practicing situations where you feel powerful. Start exercising, even just walking. Exercise and yoga connect you with your body. Group sports connect you to others. Exercise increases serotonin, which can decrease depression.

- Start by becoming aware of your feelings and needs. Then, practice small steps to express them. Do this with people you trust.

Tips for Codependency Recovery Continued

- Begin using techniques daily to build up your self-esteem inside of you. Be grateful for your positive qualities.

- Choose to embrace your emotional traumas fully. The only way out is through.

- Begin setting personal boundaries by saying "No." Talk to friends. You may have to gain enough courage to leave a toxic relationship.

- Start expressing your feelings. This may only be in a journal or to friends.

- Practice surrendering to the reality of a situation or person. At some point, you may realize you can only change yourself. You can only do your best. Learn from your mistakes to do better next time.

Practice at least one tip daily.

The Following is a Client's Experience. It shows codependency patterns in her life and ways of recovery.

Anne is an energy healer, intuitive, and spiritual teacher. She has walked the same path as her clients. Empowering women,

15 – Codependency: How to Feel Your Best and Recover

she guides them to heal karmic patterns and dissolve deep wounds. They also transmute their darkness into Light.

My wife, Lyn, and I assisted in a phone session. We both held a safe, sacred space for the client. Lyn has the intuitive ability to see and feel. She uses this to connect with and guide the client. I held the client's energy with Lyn.

Ann: *In my session with Lyn and Michael, we explored my codependent behaviors.*

Lyn: *Ann, you suggested you want to enjoy life rather than just survive.*

Ann: *I have three children. My youngest, age two, always wants all the attention. Otherwise, he gets upset and starts screaming.*

Lyn: *I see you give your family and husband all your energy. You have no time for yourself. All the time, you take care of your family. Do you feel worthwhile as a mother?*

Ann: *Yes, at times. Sometimes, my five-year-old daughter and four-year-old son cuddle on the couch together. Other times, I want some alone time.*

Lyn: *There is some codependency. You have to focus on your family's needs first. As a result, you have to ignore your own needs. This is the dilemma of all mothers.*

Ann: *Somedays, I want to stay in bed and hide under the covers.*

Lyn: *This is physical and emotional exhaustion.*

Ann: *Sometimes my husband comes home tired from work. I feel guilty when I am depleted from the kids all day. I have no energy for him.*

Lyn: *You have choices. You can feel guilty, or you can enjoy being a mom. Enjoy your kid's laughter, playfulness, and innocence. Connect with like-minded mothers for support—practice exercising, meditating, or reading a book for a few minutes each day. Be grateful for what you have. You don't live in a third-world country.*

Ann: *Thank you. Yes, it is all about my attitude.*

Lyn: *I want to point something else out to you. As a mother, you hold the Heart of the family. You hold the heart/hearth of your home. You set the mood. It can be a good or a depressing atmosphere. You set the tone for everyone else. How do you handle curve balls? Your children learn from you how to handle life.*

As a mom, you give more than you get. You do this out of love. Your love is shown with hugs, clean sheets, cooked meals, and bedtime stories. **Session Ended.**

Books on Amazon:

Codependent No More: How to Stop Controlling Others and Start Caring for Yourself by Melody Beattie.

The Language of Letting Go: Daily Meditations on Codependency by Melody Beattie.

Facing Codependence: What It Is, Where It Comes From, How It Sabotages Our Lives by Pia Mellody.

Healing the Child Within Discovery and Recovery for Adult Children of Dysfunctional Families by Charles Whitfield, MD.

Workbook for *It Doesn't Start with You* by Mark Wolynn: *Your Powerful Guide to Ending the Cycle of Inherited Family Trauma.*

The Road Less Traveled by Scott Peck. He guides you through an often-painful process of change. You gain a higher level of self-understanding.

16 - Five Core Symptoms of Codependency: How to Break Free

Recovery from codependency is a lot like a growing-up process. We must learn to do the things our dysfunctional parents did not teach us. Appropriately esteem ourselves and set functional boundaries. Be aware of and acknowledge our reality. Take care of our adult needs and wants. Experience our reality moderately. ~ Pia Mellody, author of *Facing Codependency*

Symptoms of Codependency

- Difficulty experiencing appropriate levels of self-esteem.
- Difficulty setting functional boundaries.
- Difficulty owning your reality.
- Difficulty acknowledging and meeting your own needs and wants.
- Being interdependent with others.
- Difficulty experiencing and expressing your reality.

Crestor and Lombardo, in 1999, conducted a study examining codependency in a college population. Over 90 percent demonstrated some form of codependent behavior.

Codependency is common in relationships. Discover a bigger picture.

1. Codependency Symptom: Difficulty Experiencing Significant Levels of Self-Esteem

Healthy self-esteem is the internal experience of your value as a person. It comes from the inside and moves outward into relationships. You know your value even when you make a mistake or are rejected.

Self-esteem has two extremes.

In one extreme, you believe you are worthless, less than others. In the men's groups I attended, almost all the men felt less than.

Michael: *With my father, I felt invisible. He never acknowledged or talked to me."*

On the other hand, you can feel better than others. In your family, you never did anything wrong, and you were never held responsible for your actions.

In our society, self-esteem is based on external factors, such as how much money you make or what kind of car you drive. It may also depend on how well your children do in school. This type of esteem is based on "human doing." It is also based on the opinions and behavior of other people.

Some parents live vicariously through their kids. They chatter about whose kid did the best on a test or in a game.

Self-esteem comes from within yourself. It begins with your parents. They can teach you who you are rather than being valued for what you do.

Michael: *I believe my father felt empty inside. As an alcoholic, he daily reached for his bottle of rye whiskey.*

Growing up, I filled the space left by my father. In the family, I unconsciously took over the role of father. Also, as a teenager, I took on my father's low esteem. I felt the shame of being the son of a drunk. Everyone in our small farming village knew him as an alcoholic.

Your level of self-esteem affects all your relationships, including your marriage and the messages you give your children.

What is Your Level of Esteem?

"Codependents don't just wake up one day saying, "I think I'll move over into maturity and mental health." ~ Pia Mellody

2. Codependency Symptom: No Boundaries in Your Relationships

Boundaries

Is being a friend always being there when someone needs you?

Do you struggle to say "NO" when you don't want to do something? You often end up saying "YES."

Do you blame others for your emotions like anger?

Two Types of Boundaries

Internal Boundary - Do you own your feelings, thoughts, and behaviors?

External Boundary - How close do you allow others into your physical space? Do you allow them to touch you or your property?

Having a healthy external boundary lets other people know where you are in your space and where they stand with you.

Boundaries are like fences. You are the house. You decide what your fence looks like and who is allowed in. Also, when someone can come over, once inside the fence, you can control who can enter your home. Boundaries are required in healthy relationships. They protect you and others.

Four Different Types of Boundaries

"A codependent with no boundaries not only lacks protection but cannot recognize another person's right to have boundaries with the codependent. Therefore, a codependent with nonexistent boundaries moves through other people's boundaries, unaware that he or she is doing something inappropriate." ~ Pia Mellody

1. No Boundaries: There is no protection from any kind of physical, emotional, or sexual abuse.

2. Damaged Boundaries: *"Damaged boundaries could cause a person to take responsibility for someone else's feelings, thinking, or behavior, such as when a wife feels shame and guilt because her husband insulted someone at a party."* ~ Pia Mellody

It has holes in it that confuse me. You set boundaries, and then you say "NO" to some people and not to others. Do you fully see someone's fence?

3. Walls Instead of Boundaries: *"Substitutes for an intact boundary and is most often made up of either anger or fear."* ~ Pia Mellody

Have you ever felt stone-walled or bulldozed by someone? Someone who embodies a wall of anger gives a clear message: "If you come near me or mention that, I'm going to explode." The same goes for fear. Do you retreat, stay small, or isolate to feel safe?

For example, as a teenager, I would attend a dance. I was a wallflower. Out of fear, I would sit back and watch. I had such low esteem that I feared rejection by whatever girl I asked.

4. Moving Back and Forth from Walls to No Boundaries: *"The sad thing about walls is that although they give solid protection, they do not allow for intimacy. They leave the codependent even more isolated and lonely."* ~ Pia Mellody

When you feel vulnerable, do you retreat behind a wall?

Walls protect you if you are suffering from abuse. They become dysfunctional when you want to connect with someone.

What set of boundaries do you engage in?

3. Codependency Symptom: Difficulty Owning Your Reality

Growing up, were you abandoned, attacked, or ignored? Do you struggle with accepting your reality?

Michael: *In my twenties, I had difficulty accepting the reality of one situation. My father fought almost all the time with my mother. In his drunkenness, he would yell and demean my mother.*

One day, I was visiting, and the parents were fighting. My younger brother said, "I am going to shoot that "so and so." My brother had a twenty-two rifle in his hands. Without thinking, I grabbed it from him.

There were stories of fathers in farm families killing their families. It scared me.

For many years, I wiped that memory out. The reality of the situation terrified me.

Difficulty Owning Your Reality

The difficulty manifests in two ways: Level A involves knowing your reality. However, you may choose not to own it for fear of abandonment or rejection.

Level B is not knowing your reality and thus being unable to express it. This is dysfunctional, and it means choosing to live in delusion.

Know your feelings as good. You can trust them.

Most of you probably struggle due to a traumatic childhood.

Your thoughts are good. Feelings can be trusted. Know your body never lies.

4. Codependency Symptom: Difficulty Acknowledging and Meeting Your Own Needs and Wants. Being Interdependent with Others

"As adults, our basic dependency needs are food, shelter, clothing, and medical/dental attention. Also, we need physical and emotional nurturing, sex, education, and financial resources." ~ Pia Mellody

Do you get confused between needs and wants? Food is required to survive. Wants are desires we can live without, like having a second car.

We all are dependent. For instance, kids rely on their caregivers to teach them about needs and wants. They need their caregivers to keep them safe. Eventually, the kids will be able to identify their own needs and wants. They learn how to seek out others through interdependence to help them.

Four Main Categories of Struggling to Identify Your Needs and Wants.

1. Too Dependent.
2. Anti-dependent.
3. Needless and Wantless.
4. Confusing Your Needs and Wants.

Where Do These Dysfunctional Processes Come From?

I AM Too Dependent

Do you know your needs and wants? Are you relying on others to meet them for you? Did your parents do everything for you as a Helicopter parent?

I AM Anti-Dependent

Do you want no help from anyone? Can you trust no one? Do you believe you have to fend for yourself?

I AM Needless and Wantless

"You have needs and wants. However, you are clueless as to what they are. You may have been abused, abandoned, or neglected as a child. In addition, your caregiver never met your needs and wants. As an adult, you are always meeting other people." ~ Pia Mellody

I Get My Needs and Wants Confused

Growing up, did you get what you wanted? Was this rather than what you needed?

Children need time with their parents. They need a sense of belonging and emotional nurturing. They also need to do activities together and have playtime.

"Not tending to one's needs and wants appropriately is often connected to a feeling of low self-esteem. Whenever the "adult child" feels needy or has a want, shame flares at the onset of the experience. The adult codependent feels as if he or she is terribly selfish to need or want something." ~ Pia Mellody

Michael: *My parents were poor growing up. I never felt I could ask for anything that I wanted. If I asked my mother for something, I felt guilty.*

My mother used to say, "Look at all I have done for you kids." One time, as a teenager, I asked for a school jacket. My mother bought it for me.

Know that your needs and wants matter. It may be difficult to know what they are, and you may not know how to get them. You get them through interdependence.

5. Codependency Symptom: Difficulty Experiencing and Expressing Your Reality in Moderation

16 – Five Core Symptoms of Codependency: How to Break Free

"My experience leads me to believe that operating in extremes may come from at least two situations. One is observing and reacting to the behavior of the caregivers who operate in extremes. The other is from the experience of 'not being heard' or feeling invisible in the family of origin." ~ Pia Mellody

Michael: *In my family, I became invisible. My alcoholic father blasted my mother with his anger. I retreated inward to avoid his rage. Keeping quiet to stay safe, I never expressed my feelings or thoughts. I always felt ashamed of my family and my father's drinking.*

Inward, I became invisible, the 'Lost Child.' I felt overwhelmed.

After farm chores, I spent time in nature. I played in the maple trees and walked the fields. I also learned to play the guitar and read books.

I hid my thoughts even from my mother. She assumed I was okay because I had never expressed anything.

As an adult, I wore a stoic stone face as a mask, as if I were okay. My heart had become as numb as stone.

It isn't easy to know what you're feeling and express it moderately. This key symptom affects your body, thinking, feelings, and behavior.

Body

The ability to be moderate with your body can show up in a number of ways, from being thin to being overweight.

Thinking

This is most present in people who are black and white in their thinking. There is little to "NO" room for grey. These people are either completely into something or completely out of it. There is no middle ground.

Behavior

One word extreme. Trusting everyone or trusting no one. Allowing everyone to touch them or so locked down that no one can touch them. They oscillate from one extreme to the other. There is no middle ground.

Feelings

These people either feel all the feelings or they feel no feelings at all.

Pia Mellody has identified four types of emotional experiences.

People Struggling with Codependency Face:

1. Adult Feeling Reality

Adults who experience emotions are very centered within themselves. They can clearly identify their emotions, and they know how to express them in moderation.

2. Adult-Induced Feeling Reality

Feelings come about through empathy. They feel the pain and without it overwhelming them. Furthermore, they never take the pain on themselves.

3. Frozen Feelings from Childhood

Feelings come from the need to survive. To survive trauma, they shut down. It leaves them with suppressed emotions. The frozen feelings include anger, fear, and pain.

Michael: *In my experience working with clients, the inner child always resists. The child wants to be in control and feel safe. I have the child climb into a "Tree House" where they can feel safe.*

Brene Brown states, *"You cannot selectively numb certain feelings. Numb one, you numb them all."* Brene Brown, American professor and author. She is known for her work on shame, vulnerability, and leadership.

4. Adult-to-Child Carried Feelings

The adult has absorbed all their childhood feelings of anger, fear, rage, sadness, or shame. They feel out of control and overwhelmed.

Michael: *I find my clients carry these feelings. My wife and I assist them in connecting with their inner child. We assist the adult and child to clear their feelings and shift their energies.*

It is powerful to identify your emotional experiences. Connecting to your feelings and body, healing begins.

How Can Therapy Help?

1. Therapy can help you identify and understand your thoughts and feelings. You can start coping with them.

2. Therapy can help you develop coping strategies for dealing with stress and difficult situations. You can start managing stress. This includes mindfulness and relaxation methods. There is also cognitive-behavioral therapy (CBT). CBT is a type of psychotherapy that uses practical self-help strategies. It may help you change unhealthy thinking, feeling, and behaving habits.

3. Therapy can help you improve your relationships. Relationships improve by learning how to communicate, developing strong emotional bonds, and effectively resolving conflicts.

4. Therapy can help you achieve your goals, including improving self-esteem, managing chronic health conditions, and overcoming fears.

5. Therapy can help you improve your overall well-being with the right therapist and approach.

17 - Codependency: 12 Steps and Tips - How to Best Recover

> *Hypervigilant and fear of losing control. You live in a state of readiness for attack. You feel jumpy and are easily startled. You have attacks of sudden fear or panic. You fear losing control. Codependents control, and those who caretake have been controlled.* ~ John Bradshaw, author of *The Family*

Being in a state of hypervigilance describes one aspect of my childhood codependency.

Briefly, as a codependent, you:

- Put other's needs before your own.
- Deny your feelings and needs.
- Your self-esteem depends on how well you take care of others.

I share the stories of two authors of codependent books. They both experienced challenges in childhood. As adults, they managed to overcome their codependency.

John Bradshaw's Codependency

"As a child, John had to face the challenges of an alcoholic father. His mother suffered severe depression."

Bradshaw's interest in psychology and personal development stemmed from his own experiences. He grew up in a dysfunctional family. Also, for a time, he experienced an addiction to alcohol.

These early experiences shaped his lifelong commitment. He explored the impact of family dynamics on individuals for healing.

Melody Beattie's Codependency

A single mother raised her and knew nothing about feelings.

Melody Beattie, *"By age four, we were adults. Every time I expressed a feeling, someone would say, 'Don't feel that.'"*

At age twelve, she started drinking alcohol. Before long, it was to the point of blacking out. After high school, she became a drug addict.

She started burglarizing drug stores to support her habit. Eventually, she was caught and sent to a residential drug addict rehabilitation program.

She was in a six-week program for eight months before she "got better."

Melody became aware of her codependency years later. She states:

"Within minutes of meeting a man, I was sure I'd met my soulmate. A few hours later, I would fantasize about my wedding."

"Many of us didn't know about self-care. It wasn't written about in books or talked about in school."

In Melody Beattie book, *Codependent No More:*

"I know when to say no and when to say yes. I take responsibility for my choices. The victim? She went somewhere else. The only one who can truly victimize me is myself. Ninety-nine percent of the time, I choose not to do that anymore. I continue to remember the key principles."

These principles are boundaries and expressing feelings. They also include forgiving and loving yourself.

My Codependency

I developed codependency behaviors to cope with my father's drinking. Constant fighting occurred between my father and mother.

I never felt safe expressing my thoughts and feelings. So I retreated inward and became invisible, the lost child.

I hid my thoughts even from my mother. She assumed I was okay because I had never said anything to the contrary.

As an adult, my relationships involved codependency behaviors. I remained unaware of this until my early 40's. In these relationships, I avoided expressing any feelings for fear of rejection.

My Codependency Recovery

I began my codependency recovery in the late 80's.

I read John Bradshaw's Homecoming: Reclaiming and Championing Your Inner Child and Melody Beattie book Codepen-dent No More.

I recognized my codependency. For the next twenty years, I had less and less codependency behavior.

I can see codependency as an addiction because I relied on my female partners to feel for me. This was rather than knowing and expressing my own feelings.

- *I now love myself, and I accept others as they are.*
- *I am in touch with and express my feelings.*
- *I confirm myself rather than searching outside myself for a relationship to feel okay.*
- *I am in a loving relationship. This allows me to grow into the powerful person I AM.*

Codependency Recovery

Do you want to escape childhood behavior patterns of codependency? You can learn conscious choices to transform your life.

Do you or someone you know still have a degree of codependency?

Codependency 12 Steps and Tips to Recovery

"Codependency is a condition wherein one has no inner life. Happiness is on the outside. Good feelings and self-validation lie

on the outside. They can never be generated from within." ~ John Bradshaw

These steps and tips come from the work of John Bradshaw, author of The Family.

1. Do You Feel Worthless?

- Are you a perfectionist or a controller?
- Are you out of control with your life?
- Do you fear to show your needs?
- Are you a people pleaser?

Tip for Recovery: Start becoming aware of your feelings and needs. Practice expressing your feelings with people you trust.

2. Do You Overreact?

- Does your self-esteem come from others approving of you?
- Do you constantly find needy people to take care of?
- Do you seek happiness outside of yourself?

Tip for Recovery: Begin using techniques daily to build up your self-esteem inside. Feel good about your inner qualities.

3. Do You Avoid Facing Your Inner Emotional Pain?

- Avoid pain through addictions like alcohol, depression, drugs, overeating, etc.
- Do you fall into the victim trap of hopelessness?
- Deny the truth of your reality?
- Do you isolate yourself from people?

Tip for Recovery: Choose to fully embrace, face, and go through your emotional traumas. The only way out is through.

4. Do You Experience Extremes?

- Trust everyone or no one?
- Are you all or nothing, e.g., sweet or abusive?
- Do you have no opinions, or are you critical or judgmental?
- Perceive everything as either black or white?

Tip for Recovery: Be willing to open your mind, expand your perception, and experience the gray area between black and white.

5. Do You Tolerate Increasing Intolerable Behavior?

- Are you growing more addicted to something or someone?
- Do you continue staying in an abusive relationship?
- Are you becoming physically or emotionally sick because of an unhealthy relationship?

Tip for Recovery: Begin setting personal boundaries by saying "No." Talk to friends. You may have to gain enough courage to leave a relationship.

6. Do You Practice Emotional Repression?

- Do you often feel numb or unaware of what you feel?
- Do you seldom express your feelings?

- Do you sometimes have outbursts of rage or panic attacks?

Tips for Recovery: Start by becoming aware and expressing your feelings. You can also journal or talk to friends.

7. Do You Live in Your Head?

- Do you figure everything out?
- Do you think about your problems rather than taking action?
- Do you worry a lot?
- Do you obsess over details?

Tip for Recovery: Begin to trust yourself. Become aware of what you feel in your body. Your body never lies. Begin to trust your first impressions, your heart, and your intuition.

8. Do You Tend to be Willful?

- Do you use your personal will to make something happen?
- Do you find yourself wanting to control others or events?
- Do you experience difficulty making decisions?

Tip for Recovery: Practice slowly at first. Surrender to the reality of a situation. You may realize you can only change yourself.

You can only do your best and learn from your mistakes to improve next time.

9. Enmeshed Boundaries

- Your personal emotional boundaries entangle with another person.
- You lack awareness of your needs, e.g., being tired or hungry.
- You expect others to know your feelings and needs.
- You give up on yourself.
- You strive to live up to others' expectations.
- You need to always be in a relationship or avoid relationships.

Tip for Recovery: Start to become aware of your feelings and needs. Express your feelings and needs.

10. Self-centered or Extreme Need for Admiration

- You use your children to give you love.
- Outer acclaim and possessions make you feel worthwhile.
- No amount of acclaim and love is ever enough.
- You seek relationships with people who feel they need you.

Tip for Recovery: Find a good inner child therapist. Begin healing your childhood wounds.

11. Poor Communication Skills

- You have difficulty saying or knowing what you mean.
- You believe what you say as being unimportant.
- You make indirect rather than direct remarks.

- People's verbal and nonverbal signals confuse you.

Tip for Recovery: Take training to improve your communication skills.

12. Feeling Disconnected

- You feel depressed a lot.
- You feel like life has no meaning.
- You feel powerless to change your life; you feel like a victim.
- You seldom feel connected to others.

Tip for Recovery: Learn grounding exercises to connect to the earth. Start seeing and practicing situations where you feel powerful.

Start exercising, even just walking. Exercise increases serotonin and can decrease depression. It also connects us more with our bodies and to others through group sports.

Practice at least one or more tips daily.

18 – How To Best Deal with Stress and Overwhelm

The greatest weapon against stress is our ability to choose one thought over another. ~ William James, American Philosopher and Psychologist

Left Brain Mind Chatter

- How do you best solve your life's problems?
- What percentage of time do you spend in left brain thinking?
- What percentage of you feel overwhelmed and stressed out?
- Do you believe you're unable to stop your constant mind chatter? You can with the right tools and practice.

Non-cognitive Information

"*Nine-tenths of the information we're exposed to each day is non-cognitive.*" ~ The Seer Almine, Mystic

Non-cognitive relates to your right brain.

This involves other states of knowing, communication between the subconscious and higher consciousness, and information revealing itself through feelings and meditation practice.

Revelation also occurs through symbols in nature. These symbols involve totem animals and birds, insects, clouds, etc. Symbols in your subconscious show up in dreams.

Dysfunctional Stress

1. Ignore problems: Sweep them under the rug. This creates dysfunctional homes and relationships. Seventy-eight percent to eighty percent of Americans consider their families dysfunctional (Gourani, 2019).

Dysfunction may also produce physical illness.

Trauma is often at the heart of your emotional dis-tress. Emotional childhood wounds or acute adult stress are big factors in anxiety. These also present in stress, depression, addiction, anger, and suppression. Soldering on with these conditions hurts your body.

"Seventy percent of Americans are on at least one prescription drug; more than half take two." Myth of Normal by Gabor Mate, MD

"55% of Americans stress during the day." The American Institute of Stress 2022.

2. The average person tackles the problem head-on, attempting to think it through. They see the problem through their limited world perception.

18 – How to Best Deal with Stress and Overwhelm

Michael: *My experience shows learning hides within a problem. I experience evolving through challenges.*

A More Consciousness Way to Solve Problems

- You can connect to the power around you in your environment, nature, and the Divine.
- Acknowledge the problem exists.
- Then surrender it to the Divine.
- When you completely surrender, answers arise at their own timing.
- Stay aware of the symbols/signs of nature around you.
- Be aware of your feelings.
- In the silence of your mind/meditation, answers arise.
- Requires little effort.

A Way of Solving Problems with Dream Symbols

Your subconscious presents the language of dream symbols. For example, an owl may represent seeing into the dark. Also, look at what feelings or thoughts the owl stirs up. Medicine animals appear when you're ready to integrate their medicine/qualities.

Top Stress Management Tips: How to Best Increase Physical and Emotional Health

"Stress is hurting our physical and emotional health. It also contributes to some of the leading causes of death in this country."
~ American Psychological Association, 2010

You all experience stress. Sometimes, you have more tension with a given particular situation or people. Although you have no control over what happens to you, you have a choice. You can choose how you act in these situations. This is instead of reacting and feeling frazzled.

Top Stress Management Tips

1. Breathe Deeply

Do you breathe shallow and unconsciously?

- Begin by putting your hand on your abdomen below the navel.
- Inhale slowly through your nose and watch your hand move out as your belly expands as you breathe. Hold your breath for a few seconds, and then exhale slowly as you push the belly in as far as possible.
- Repeat several times.

Breathing from your diaphragm increases oxygen in your blood. This relaxes you and decreases stress.

2. Anchoring: Visualize or Imagine a Positive Calming Scene

- When you learn this method, you can relive the experience of feeling good and calm.
- Sit comfortably.

- Close your eyes and relax your body by breathing deeply into areas of your body. Breathe where you feel tightness or discomfort.
- Go back in time or create a place where you feel good and at peace.
- It may be a beach, a mountain valley, or a meadow with a stream. Visualize or imagine this place with all the sights, sounds, smells, and feelings.
- When you feel good and at peace, touch your thumb and 1st finger of your left and right hands together.
- Do these two more times, each time feeling good and peaceful. Visualize or imagine your peaceful place.
- Whenever you start to feel stressed, repeat the anchoring. Your stress will melt away.

3. Self-hand or Foot Massage

- Massage the sore areas in your palms or feet with your thumb and fingers on the other hand. This will release tension.
- There is a lot of tension between your thumb and 1st finger on the palm side.
- Massage until the stress decreases.
- You may actually breathe a sigh of relief.

4. Smile

- You smile when you feel happy.
- Smiling sends nerve signals to the limbic system in your brain.

- This creates a neurochemical balance of calm.
- Smiling can relax you.

5. Do Physical Stretching

- Your muscles tighten as you progress through your day. Stress seizes up your body even more.
- Stretching loosens your muscles and improves your breathing. If you notice birds, cats, and dogs, they stretch whenever their bodies feel tight.
- Apart from having a specific time to do physical exercise, you can stretch any time during the day. Do this even while sitting down or on a plane.
- It is best to get out of your chair every hour and stretch for a few minutes.
- A great stress-relieving stretch is a yoga position called the child pose. This stretches the back muscles.
- On the floor, kneel, sit back on your heels, lean forward, and put your forehead on the floor. Your arms are alongside your legs, palms up. Hold for one to three minutes.
- Stop and do the Child Pose.

6. Learn to Set Personal Boundaries and Say "No"

- When you want to say "No" and say "Yes" to your friends. You create stress for yourself.
- Codependents find it challenging to say "No." They either remain unaware of what they want. Or else they fear rejection by saying "No."

- Saying "No" to be true to yourself requires courage and practice.
- The only way to build up the strength to say "No" to taking care of yourself is to do it repeatedly until it becomes easier.

More Top Stress Management Tips

1. Increase the Energy or Chi in Your Body
- Rub your hands together until they feel warm.
- Then, cup them over your closed eyes for five seconds while you breathe deeply.
- Experience the comfort and release of stress.
- Again, rub your hands together until they feel warm.
- Then, with each hand, rub a kidney in your lower back at least 30 times.
- Experience the increase in energy and release of stress.

2. Do Self-Acupressure
- Locate, between the eyebrows, the indentation where the bridge of the nose meets the forehead.
- Massage this area with a forefinger for 1-2 minutes as you breathe out any stress.
- Also, find the hollow midway below each eyebrow. Massage each simultaneously with your forefingers for 1-2 minutes as you breathe out any stress.

- Find the left and right occipitals at the base of your skull. Massage each at the same time with your thumbs for 1-2 minutes as you breathe out any stress.
- Reach around the back and find the inside tip of the top of your left or right shoulder blade. Massage it with your forefinger for 1-2 minutes.
- Breathe deeply and apply firm, steady pressure for 1-2 minutes. Then do the other side.

3. Shake and Breathe Deeply. Stand. Stretch Your Arms Out from Your Sides. Shake Your Hands Vigorously for 10 seconds. Combine This with Deep Breathing.

Loosens the muscles in your neck and upper back tension.

4. Walk, Run, or Do Physical Exercise.

Any type of physical exercise assists you in breathing deeper. This improves circulation and eliminates toxins in your body. When you exercise, your brain produces endorphins, which create a sense of well-being. You receive extra benefits when you walk or hike in nature.

5. Call or Talk to a Friend. Write in a Journal About Your Feelings.

6. Pet a Cat or Dog

- Researchers have found that petting an animal for a few minutes relieves stress.
- If you don't owe a pet, visit a friend who does.
- Both the pet and the friend will help you.

Stress Management Tips: Seven Stress Relief Secrets

1. Embrace Your Feelings

- Rather than avoiding and pushing feelings away, learn to contain them. It's like holding a baby in your arms.

- Be present with the sensations in your body without doing anything. Over time, your feelings will transform without any effort.

- Be Here Now! Learn to live in the present rather than the past or the future. This is a new way of looking at your internal world.

- Living in the moment with all your feelings and pain becomes an acquired skill. Avoid and push your pain away. It remains an undercurrent of stress, never healing. Has that method worked for you?

In *The Power of Now*, Ekhart Tolle describes how you can develop the ability to live in the now, the present moment.

Tolle teaches you how your thoughts and emotions get in the way. Do you choose happiness or suffering?

2. Examine Your Critical Self-Talk

Become conscious of the negative things you say. Do you do this in your head over and over? Your critical self-talk creates emotional stress without relief.

Become aware of the related events, feelings, and critical self-talk.

Start reprogramming your subconscious mind with positive self-talk.

In Carolyn Ball book, *Claiming Your Self-Esteem,* she has practical steps. She helps you reprogram your thinking. Carolyn's methods help you to understand and recognize thought patterns. As a result, your self-esteem improves, and you experience stress reduction.

3. Begin Codependency Recovery

Become aware of how you give your power away for a temporary self-esteem boost. Are you a caretaker who looks after everyone except yourself?

Melody Beattie book, *Codependent No More* gives you the key to understanding codependency. She teaches you how to overcome codependency with life stories, reflections, and self-tests. Recognizing and choosing recovery frees you from the stress of abusive, unhealthy relationships.

4. Heal the Wounded Inner Child

You probably carry wounds from your childhood. Your inner child connects to your emotions.

In *Healing the Child Within,* Charles Whitfield describes our inner child lost in trauma. Recognize your inner child's voice and needs. You will experience more stress relief and happiness. When your child heals, you heal.

5. Heal the Unconscious Shadow

Carl Jung explored the shadow sides of our psyche in depth. You have a personal shadow side made up of qualities. Do you ignore yours? On a deeper level, humanity's collective shadow lurks, affecting us all. War erupts as an aspect of a national or global shadow side.

The negative parts of yourself remain buried. They continue adding to your suffering and sabotage your conscious efforts. Your relationships and life situations mirror these parts back to you daily.

"Bring your shadow parts into the light of your awareness. They heal and thereby reveal new strengths." ~ Carl Jung, author of *Archetypes and The Collective Unconscious*

6. Conscious Choice

Choose to become aware of your resistance to life. Also, look at your unconscious reactions to say "No." This resistance magnifies your stress levels.

Open to Divine Grace and miracles. Grace eases stress and suffering like sunshine melting snow.

One miracle which we take for granted is that of your body. Any unresolved emotions, such as trauma and abuse, become stored in your body. This creates stress. When you become willing to begin healing these emotions, you feel relief.

Dr. Candace Pert, a neuroscientist, *Your Body Is Your Subconscious Mind,* teaches the secret to transforming your emotions, body, and health.

7. Develop Your Strengths/Be of Service in Your Life Purpose

Follow your passion in service to others. Then your sufferings fall away.

Raise above your personality self. The stress of your personal challenges falls away.

In Dan Millman's book *The Life You Were Born to Live*, he explains your life challenges and areas of service. Also, he describes your special talents and your individual life path.

Overview

Dealing With Overwhelm and Stress

- Stopping feelings of overwhelm. Recognize the signs and understand the causes.
- Once you know what's triggering these feelings, address them.
- Simplify your schedule where possible. Set realistic goals. Take things one step at a time.
- Prioritize tasks and learn to say "NO" to unessential things.
- Focus on the present. Incorporate relaxation techniques like deep breathing, meditation, or mindfulness.
- Talk about your feelings with someone you trust. If needed, seek help from a therapist.

Books You May Want to Read:

Myth of Normal by Gabor Mate.

Claiming Your Self-Esteem, by Carolynn Ball.

The Power of Now, by Eckhart Tolle.

Healing the Child Within, by Charles Whitfield.

The Archetypes and The Collective Unconscious, by Carl Jung.

Your Body Is Your Subconscious Mind, by Candace Pert.

The Life You Were Born to Live, by Dan Millman.

19 - Spiritual Growth:
My Dark Night of the Soul

Without suffering, he (man) scarcely cares to recall that he has forsaken his eternal home. Pain is a prod to remembrance. The way to escape is through wisdom. ~ Yogananda, author of *Autobiography of a Yogi*

Lessen Suffering

Do you want to lessen your suffering? Make an effort with all your heart. This is "twenty-five percent" of the requirement. It also includes improving through inner emotional and spiritual work.

"Another twenty-five percent" involves the guidance of inner and outer teachers. This includes angels, friends, books, seminars, and healing. The "last fifty percent" involves Divine Grace. Grace surrounds us all the time as a part of creation." - Yogananda

Michael: *In 1994, I experienced a Dark Night of the Soul. It lasted for a number of months. Feeling utterly alone, I suffered disconnection from all my friends.*

I felt depressed and fatigued all the time. My Dark Night differed. Unlike the common description, I felt connected to the Divine. Never had I been this aware of the Divine in my life before. I trusted the Divine and followed its guidance without hesitation.

Catholic Mystic, Saint John of the Cross states, "*If a man wishes to be sure of the road he's traveling on, then he must close his eyes and travel in the dark.*"

Michael: *I had no need to close my eyes. My higher intuition/ Divine guided me. However, I had lost meaning in my purpose in life. A question haunted me: 'What is the purpose of my life?' I had known it before.*

Is the Dark Night and Depression the Same?

The Dark Night of the Soul differs from regular depression.

Depression shares characteristics with the experience of having a Dark Night. States of depression, however, result from chemical imbalances or unhealthy thought patterns. They also occur from mental illness or genetics.

Michael: *My depression stemmed from a lineage of genetic family depression. Growing up, depression hung over the whole family. This rose whenever my parents stopped fighting.*

The Dark Night creates a Spiritual Depression. There is no cure. No one can save you. Only you can save yourself.

You never know when the Dark Night will end. Eventually, a Light will appear at the end of the tunnel.

Deep-seated spiritual changes occur in a Dark Night. You will feel excitement again.

19 – Spiritual Growth: My Dark Night of the Soul

Seven Possible Signs of the Dark Night

1. Deep sadness.

2. Feeling unworthy.

3. Lost in a life of suffering.

4. Powerlessness.

5. A challenge to take action.

6. No joy or excitement.

7. Long for change to a former life.

Why Suffering/Strengthening is Necessary?

"Without passing through very difficult experiences ... we cannot understand human beings. We cannot realize our multi-dimensional and multilevel development toward higher and higher levels." ~ Kazimierz Dabrowski, author of *Positive Disintegration*

The theory of positive disintegration (TPD) is an idea of personality development. Polish psychologist Kazimierz Dąbrowski developed it. This psychology is unlike mainstream psychology. The theory views psychological tension as necessary for personal growth.

"My desire to live is as intense as ever. Though my heart is broken, hearts are made to be broken. That is why God sends sorrow into the world... To me, suffering now seems a sacramental thing. It makes those whom it touches holy... any materialism in life coarsens the soul." ~ Oscar Wilde, Irish Poet and Playwright

A Dark Night can't be fixed. Neither is it a badge of honor.

Michael: *My Dark Night had a lasting impact. Although my former meaning of life may have been taken away, my meaning became stronger.*

Have you ever seen a butterfly begin to emerge from its cocoon? It struggles to strengthen its wings. If it is freed, the butterfly emerges from its cocoon prematurely, unable to fly.

The tempering stage is necessary for strengthening. Trees also need wind in order to build their structural strength and stay upright.

What is the Point of Living?

This question arises in The Dark Night. It also arises in daily life.

There are multiple answers. Are you to serve yourself or to serve others? Perhaps you're to serve a higher purpose or the Divine? Despair sets in when every path turns out meaningless or empty.

Michael: *My mind was unable to figure out the answer. As I said before, my Higher Intuition/Divine guided me. My mind always wanted to figure everything out.*

Suffering and the Dark Night of the Soul

"Through every trial, we grow. All suffering we experience has a meaning. Though it seems very cruel, it is like the fire that smelts the iron ore. The steel that emerges from that furnace is beautifully strong, useful for many purposes." ~ Yogananda

Yogananda, an Indian yogi, introduced the Western world to meditation and Kriya yoga for self-realization. You may suffer from life or a Dark Night of the Soul.

Yogananda explains how to achieve liberation, which also means freedom from suffering. He describes three ways to overcome emotional pain and suffering. Then, you receive Divine Grace.

Divine Grace

- Grace involves complete surrender.
- Surrender of your mind and fears.
- Letting go of physical and mental suffering. You suffer because of what you believe is "Truth."

Allowing Divine Grace to come in any form.

Michael: *In my Dark Night, my Higher Intuition or Divine Grace guided me.*

Divine Grace Lessening Suffering

"All surrendering love draws His Grace." ~ Yogananda

Conclusion: Healing Emotional Pain with Divine Grace

- Stay present with feelings in your body. Your body never lies. It lets you know the reality at the moment.
- It takes practice to stay present. You have been taught to push away discomfort.
- Does your mind take you into the past or future? You may even want to escape your body.

- Pain only dissolves when you remain connected to it. Your surrender opens the space for the Grace. Then, the Grace dissolves the pain. It requires no effort.

- You need to be willing to reveal false beliefs. Do you want to stay angry and blame someone? Instead, you could feel the anger within you.

- Now, choose to look up into the face of Grace. It shines like sunlight from above. Allow Grace into the heart of your pain.

Experiences of the Dark Night of the Soul

Tom: *It has been a roller coaster of extreme highs and lows. I have learned so much on my continued Dark Night. I understand myself more. Integrating my dark side is crucial for me. When I hid it, others manipulated me. I have much to learn. Life is a constant school of learning.*

Lesley: *I experienced a Dark Night of the Soul. My twin flame cheated and left me. He was also abusive. I entered the depths of a Dark Night. In the Dark Night, I experienced insomnia, panic attacks, and suicidal thoughts. Everything felt like a dream. I felt disconnected from everything and everyone. Before, I used to feel so connected. The Divine has been letting me know over and over that I am being healed. I need to trust the process even though I want to resist. It is better, yet I am so disconnected from the Divine Source.*

Erica: *I experienced a Dark Night of the Soul once. Something was wrong with the pregnancy. My husband and I faced a situation where there was no control. We couldn't change it. I was expecting* *twin boys. It was a desperate and painful time. Everything in my life came tumbling down. My spiritual foundation crumbled. I received only a deafening silence to my prayers. I honestly felt like there was some kind of spiritual battle going on. The battle was for my soul and the souls of my sons. The end finally came. It was a brutal experience like no other I have ever experienced. I will never forget it. The Dark Night of the Soul is reserved for spiritual seekers. Today, I have two beautiful boys. Take heart.*

A destruction process must occur before any true growth or healing can occur. A complete annihilation of everything you thought would bring you happiness.

Six steps that identify and change thoughts and emotions held in your body. This will teach you to stay present with feelings in your body. Eugene Gendlin, author of *Focusing*.

20 - Embodying Divine Male and Female Archetypes for Better Health

The collective unconscious consists of the sum of the instincts and their correlates, the archetypes. Just as everybody possesses instincts, so he also possesses a stock of archetypal images. ~ Carl Jung

Archetypes

1. The archetype energies exist in all of us. You can harness them for personal growth.
2. These archetypes can be integrated.
3. They show up in relationships and work.
4. Each archetype has a shadow or subconscious side. If imbalanced, it can lead to destructive behaviors.
5. You can develop the archetypes for higher consciousness and spiritual growth.

Archetypes: Symbols of Higher States of Consciousness

You have qualities of female and male goddesses and gods within you. Their stories describe higher and lower states of consciousness.

These stories live in our collective consciousness. You see the archetypes in books and films. They show up in your relationships and work.

The Male energy connects to your left brain, which is on the right side of your body. The Male focuses on logic, the mind, and accomplishing a task.

The Female energy connects to the right brain on the left side of your body. It shows up as creativity, intuition, and nurturing.

Both sides need to be balanced for your health.

The Divine Female has qualities of nurturing, compassion, and healing.

Historical Goddesses

Venus/Aphrodite Greek and Roman – Goddess of Love and Beauty.

Minerva/Athena Roman and Greek – Goddess of Wisdom and Strategy.

Ceres/Demeter Roman and Greek – Goddess of Harvest and Agriculture.

Diana/Artemis Roman and Greek – Goddess of the Hunt and Moon.

Proserpina/Persephone Roman and Greek – Queen of the Underworld.

Morrigan Irish – Goddess of Battle and War.

Kali Hindu – protector and destroyer of ignorance.

Modern Day Spiritual Women

Amma – Indian Hugging Saint.

Mother Meera – gives Darshan/Blessings.

Anandamayi Ma – India Saint and Mystic.

Exploring the Archetypes of the Divine Feminine

The following quotes are by Sylvia Salow, healer, speaker, and author.

"The divine masculine energy wants the goddess energy within women. It's the limitless creative energy itself that is mesmerizing, magnetic, and potent."

"You have that power within. It's always been there, waiting for you to tap into it."

"One of the most common ways women unconsciously strip themselves of their inner power is to ensure love in a romantic relationship. They often feel they must choose between being loved and tapping into the limitless creative power within."

"The true role of feminine power is the ability to birth something that never existed to this planet, to give form to a spiritual energy, to be so connected to your vision and to your inner knowing that you create from that inner knowing, even if it doesn't make logical sense or if others have different opinions. A powerful woman gives birth to herself."

Divine Feminine Archetypes: *"We women, when we're searching for a meaning to our lives or for the path of knowledge, always identify with one of four classic archetypes."* ~ Paulo Coelho

A Divine Feminine Archetype exhibits the best and highest expression of these energies in a woman.

Divine Feminine Archetype qualities emerge more as women begin taking their rightful place with men in the world to balance the masculine energies ruling the world at this time.

Each of you, both men and women, carry Divine Masculine and Divine Feminine Archetype energies within your psyche. You manifest these energies in your everyday activities. By consciously developing these qualities, you become more mature and balanced as men and women working together for a better world for all.

Men, I challenge you to become aware and integrate the feminine archetype qualities into your inner feminine or anima.

What Six Divine Feminine Archetypes Do Women Possess?

Notice what qualities you possess in each of the archetypes to see your strengths; also, at the end of the article, notice where you can develop more as you read the questions related to the shadow aspects of the archetype.

Goddess/Creatrix Archetype: A Creatrix produces new creations. Unlike the other archetypes, a Goddess/Creatrix functions as a higher spiritual aspect in some women. Rather than being developed, it functions as a natural aspect of their true spiritual being.

At a certain level of consciousness, a woman recognizes this Goddess/Creatrix, which begins working through her, allowing her to create new manifestations in her career, finances, and life. A Goddess/Creatrix contains qualities of the other archetypes.

- Connects with the flow of life.
- Creates new possibilities.
- Originates new ideas.
- Possesses intuitive wisdom.
- Radiates unconditional love.
- Rejuvenates and heals those she influences.

Queen/Leader Archetype: Selfless and Wise – Incorporates the Lover, Mother and Warrior. Authors, humanitarians, mystics, politicians, queens, saints, and scientists

- Accepts reality – lives in the present.
- Embodies the full potential of life.
- Experiences from the heart rather than the mind.
- Her life and spiritual path are the same.
- Knows the unity of life.
- Lives in service for others.
- Realizes everything is sacred.

Lover Archetype: Passionate About Life and Sensitive

- A romantic.
- Brings together the duality of the male and female energies.
- Compassionate and kind.

- Connected with emotions/emotionally intelligent.
- Creative, playful, and sensual.
- Experiences life in the moment.
- Loves contact and connection.

Mother Archetype: Provides a Domain of Loving Care

- Caring and compassionate.
- She holds the center of happiness and well-being for her household.
- Loving selflessly.
- Persistent.
- Nurturers.
- Stabilizing influence.

Priestess Archetype: Intuitive Awareness into the Unknown

- Awareness of other dimensions/realms.
- Conduit for healing energies.
- Grounded in her body.
- High discernment.
- Listens to her heart and body wisdom.
- Searches for higher knowledge.

Warrioress/Amazon Archetype: Stands and Fights for the Truth.

- Assertive.
- Athletic.

- Completes tasks.
- Courageous.
- Maintains good personal boundaries.
- Protects the innocent and the inner child.

Now that you recognize your Feminine Archetypes, what Archetypes of your Divine Feminine would you like to develop more?

Asking and finding solutions to the following applicable questions will assist your development.

The questions relate to the unconscious, undeveloped wounded parts, i.e., your shadow aspects, which irritate you when you see them in others.

"Everything that irritates us about others can lead us to an understanding of ourselves." ~ Carl Jung

Healing the Shadow Aspects of Your Divine Feminine Archetype

Answer the questions for the following Archetypes in a notebook.

Goddess/Creatrix Divine Feminine Archetype:

- How do I manipulate others?
- Am I paranoid?
- Do I doubt myself or the Divine?

Action: Discover and heal the core of your self-doubt. This takes time.

Mother Divine Feminine Archetype:

- How can I heal the wounds of my own mother?
- How can I learn to nurture myself instead of exhausting myself by constantly nurturing everyone else?
- Am I codependent, and how do I become less codependent?

Action: Find a good healer or therapist to heal your wounds. Get a workbook on overcoming codependency or join a codependency recovery group.

Queen Divine Feminine Archetype:

- What is the fear behind my desire to overcontrol others?
- Do I need to learn to love myself more?

Action: Meditate daily to develop your spiritual being. Let go of your inner stories that keep you from suffering. See a healer or therapist to learn to stay with the feelings and sensations in your body, even resistance.

Priestess Divine Feminine Archetype:

- Where am I over-subjective in my life?
- Is it difficult for me to be in my body and grounded?

Action: Ask a question from your heart and then walk in nature to experience your body and nature.

Lover Divine Feminine Archetype:

- Does my inner child/little girl need to be seen and loved?
- Am I self-absorbed?
- Am I more concerned about outer rather than inner beauty?
- Do I have a distorted body image?
- Where am I insensitive to the needs of others? When do I compare myself to others?
- Do I manipulate others to get what I want?

Action: Find a healer or a therapist to heal the wounds of abuse and trauma. Learn about personal boundaries. Indulge in healthy ways to nurture yourself.

Warrioress Divine Feminine Archetype:
- Where do I create chaos, drama, or fits of anger or jealousy?
- Where do I withhold love?
- Who do I need to forgive?

Action: Ask your inner child what she needs. Write a letter to your inner child. Then, with your opposite hand, have your inner child write a letter back to you. Learn to ask for what you need.

Embodying Divine Masculine Archetypes

"Man is originally characterized by his 'search for meaning' rather than his 'search for himself.' The more he forgets himself—giving

himself to a cause or another person—the more human he is. And the more he is immersed and absorbed in something or someone other than himself, the more he really becomes himself." ~ Viktor E. Frankl

Frankl delves into the paradox of self-identity and purpose. It's not in the pursuit of their own image that mankind truly comes into being. It's in the surrender to something greater. They find their true essence by losing themselves in the cosmic tapestry of life.

Lover:

The lover archetype signifies passion, creativity, and the ability to connect deeply with others and the world. It represents the individual's capacity to experience joy, affection, and pleasure.

The Lover is not just limited to romantic love but encompasses a broader spectrum of emotions and connections, including self-love and love for humanity.

Warrior:

The Warrior archetype embodies the strength, courage, and determination necessary to confront challenges and protect what is valuable.

It represents the individual's capacity to take decisive action, persevere in adversity, and uphold their values.

The true Warrior acts with integrity, seeking justice and maintaining a sense of honor.

Magician:

The Magician archetype is associated with wisdom and intuition. It is a deep understanding of the mysteries of life. It represents the capacity for introspection, self-reflection, and transformative growth. The Magician possesses the ability to tap into the unconscious and heal wounds. He manifests a desired change in oneself and the world.

King:

The King archetype symbolizes sovereignty and the ability to lead with wisdom, empathy, and responsibility.

It represents the individual's capacity to set healthy boundaries and make competent decisions. They create a nurturing environment for themselves and others.

The King also embodies a sense of purpose and the ability to guide others towards their full potential.

King/Leader Qualities:

- Benevolent, calm, and intelligent.
- Right action, selfless, stable, and wise.

Lover Qualities:

- Appreciates beauty and connects to others.
- Joy, passionate and sensitive to others.
- In his body, grounded.

Magician Qualities:

- Curious and reflective.
- Mediator.
- Possesses some manual skills.

Warrior Qualities:

- Clarity of thought.
- Decisive discipline.
- Knows himself.
- Loyal.
- Protector.
- Selfless service.

How Do You Develop the Four Divine Masculine Archetypes to Become a More Mature Man?

A more mature man has greater confidence and a sense of life purpose in selfless service to others.

King/Leader: Selfless and wise, incorporates the Lover, Magician and Warrior.

- Be decisive.
- Become a mentor.
- Develop a life plan.
- Develop traits of leadership.
- Establish core values.
- Find a mentor.
- Live with integrity.

Lover: Passionate About Life and Sensitive

- Find a hobby to be passionate about.

- Learn how to experience life in the moment with all your senses.
- Seek knowledge which fires your imagination and inspiration.
- Spend time outdoors alone connecting to nature and yourself.
- Take time to enjoy healthy pleasures.
- Take time for romance.

Magician: Master of Inner and Outer Transformation

- Becomes a mentor.
- Commits to lifelong learning.
- Creates sacred space for alone time.
- Finds identity through creating.
- Learns some manual skills.
- Meditates to develop focus and release stress.
- Takes part in rites of passage.

Warrior: To Dare and Fight for a Noble Cause

- Be decisive.
- Discover your core values.
- Discover your principles.
- Find a purpose in life.
- Learn a Martial Art.
- Strengthen disciple through daily routines.

Resources for Further Study

Way of the Peaceful Warrior: A Book That Changes Lives, by Dan Millman.

This autobiography reaches the way of the peaceful warrior. Life as a peaceful warrior is a life of meditation, mindfulness, compassion, and acceptance.

In *Way of the Peaceful Warrior,* the old man, Socrates, arouses Millman's curiosity. Dan learns the path of the peaceful warrior, a life philosophy on how to live with focus and intention.

King, Warrior, Magician, and Lover by Robert Moore and Douglas Gillette, Jungian Psychologists. This is a transformative and influential book.

Further Exploration of Archetypal Energies Archetypes: A Beginner's Guide to Your Internet, by Caroline Myss.

Myths for the Future: A Futurist Look at the Archetypes Which Guide Our Common Destiny, by Jean Houston - Audio Cassette/Audiobook, January 1, 5.

The Spontaneous Fulfillment of Desire: Harnessing the Infinite Power of Coincidence, by Deepak Chopra.

21 - Self-Growth: How to Best Start Successful Shadow Work

People will do anything, no matter how absurd, to avoid facing their own souls. One does not become enlightened by imagining figures of light but by making the darkness conscious. ~ Carl Jung, Psychology and Alchemy

Results of My Shadow Test

Michael: I have a low-level shadow self. I acknowledge and accept most parts of my nature. Rarely do I repress, reject, or condemn aspects of myself. I live a life unhindered by the shadow's self-sabotage. Over my life, I have done a lot of inner healing work. I continue practicing self-awareness, self-acceptance, and self-compassion. Still, I need to be mindful of my shadow.

Your Dark Side

Your Shadow self is a dark and mysterious place in your subconscious. You may have refused to shine the "Light" on it.

Your human Shadow contains thoughts, feelings, and personality traits. You may have rejected or suppressed them.

All of you carry Shadows inside you. You can ignore and bury their existence either out of fear or shame.

Shunning your Shadow tends to undermine and sabotage your life. Addictions, low self-esteem, and mental and chronic illness can all be caused by your Shadow.

Shadow Work assists you in experiencing deep healing.

Traditionally, Shadow Work fell into the realm of Shamans or medicine people. Priests and Priestesses also assisted in the past.

These days, Shadow Work falls into the domain of psychotherapy, which includes psychologists, psychiatrists, spiritual guides, and therapists.

You now have an opportunity to look at your Shadows. It is a path for your spiritual growth.

What is Shadow Work?

"Everyone carries a shadow, and the less it is embodied in the individual's conscious life, the blacker and denser it is." ~ Carl Jung, Psychology and Religion

The concept of the Shadow originated in the work of psychoanalyst Carl Jung.

Shadow work is the practice of finding and transmuting the wounded and suppressed parts of yourself. Then, you can regain your inner Light.

Spiritual Teacher Tolle

Eckhart Tolle referred to the Shadow archetype. He called it the "pain body."

"The pain-body, which is the dark shadow cast by the ego, is actually afraid of the light of your consciousness. It is afraid of being found out. Its survival depends on your unconscious identification with it, as well as on your unconscious fear of facing the pain that lives in you. But if you don't face it, if you don't bring the light of your consciousness into the pain, you will be forced to relive it again and again." ~ Eckhart Tolle, author of *The Power of Now*.

My Journey Towards the Shadow

Michael: *At the age of twenty-four, I knew the most important goal in my life. It involved emotional and spiritual growth.*

However, I had no idea how to accomplish that goal.

My left-brain thinking mind ran my life. I attempted to figure everything out. Inside, I felt numb all the time. I had no understanding about how to look inside myself.

I went to the Center for Feeling Therapy in Los Angeles. Then, for three years, I lived in a small community and explored my feelings weekly in therapy and small groups.

As a child, I experienced trauma and my father's anger. In my adult years, I had no sense that repressed emotions related to my Shadow.

So, the Feeling Therapy moved me toward of healing my Shadow. I have been on that journey ever since.

Do We All Have a Shadow Self?

Yes, the Shadow is your family conditioning. You have a Shadow even though you see yourself as a "good person."

No exceptions exist, even if you are generous and loving.

As a human, you possess both a Light and a Dark side. Embrace that reality in this three-dimensional world.

You may believe only criminals, murderers, and thieves have a Shadow side.

Black-and-white thinking is a major cause of your suffering.

Do You Have These Perceptions?

- Criminals, murderers, and thieves are less than human.
- I am better than other people.
- I am a model citizen.
- I should be applauded for all my good deeds.
- I have very few bad thoughts.

These perceptions ignore your Shadow side.

How is Your Shadow Side Formed?

Your Shadow Side is formed in childhood. You learned to behave in a certain way to be accepted.

Michael: *For example, my family showed little warmth, i.e., no hugs. I became self-sufficient and developed my mind.*

My Shadow remained in my unconscious. I was completely unaware of it. However, it did appear in my teenage years. It showed up as low self-esteem and taking on blame for my father's alcoholism. I also felt ashamed of having my father's last name.

My father had a lot of anger. I also had a lot of anger, which I repressed. My mother could have taught me healthy ways of expressing anger. However, she had no training herself growing up.

I learned how to survive by staying quiet. To this day, I would rather have peace than conflict in my relationships.

Other People's Shadow Work Experiences

Melody: *I have been fighting with my Shadow self for some time now. Also, I believe this journey starts without knowing what is going on. It goes back and forth. I have been in what feels like a never-ending battle. On many occasions, I felt like I was drowning. I never really knew how to address the issues—until today, when I truly discovered that I have a dark side. I am ready to confront and surrender to this side of me.*

Brigid: *I have learned to acknowledge my Shadow. By doing so, I have gained the ability to respond instead of react. Instead of fighting it, I welcome it. My Shadow reveals who I choose to be. I have learned I can never rid myself of my Shadow. Attempting to gives it greater power. I accept it as an ally, a friend, and a teacher. This allows me to live above it.*

Mary: *I have dark thoughts about religion. I was raised in a religious Christian background. I went to church on Sundays and Wednesdays for my entire childhood and high school years. A lot* *of scary thoughts and the fear of being possessed have come up. I am starting to think I may have a Shadow in my subconscious. In my conditioning, I believe in black-and-white, good and bad. What keeps my fear at bay is the belief that there must be Light where there is Darkness.*

To fit in, did you learn to act in a certain way? Did you adopt certain roles to ensure your physical, emotional, and mental survival?

Carl Jung once stated, *"The Shadow is ninety percent pure gold."* This means there are many beautiful gifts offered to us by our Shadow side.

Steve Wolf, Therapist, states, *"We seek to present a beautiful, innocent face to the world... And so, unknowingly but inevitably, we push away those qualities that do not fit the image. These do not enhance our self-esteem and make us stand proud. Instead, they bring us shame and make us feel small. But while the Shadow Self may be portrayed as our 'evil twin,' it is not entirely full of 'bad.'"*

Final Inspiring Shadow Work Quotes

"The secret is out: all of us, no exceptions, have qualities we won't let anyone see. This includes our Shadow. If we face up to our dark side, our life can be energized. If not, there is the devil to pay. This is one of life's most urgent projects." ~ Larry Dossey, author of *Healing Words*

"To honor and accept one's own shadow is a profound spiritual discipline. It is whole-making and thus holy and the most important experience of a lifetime." ~ Robert Johnson

"To confront a person with his own shadow is to show him his own Light." ~ Carl Jung

What Happens When You Reject Your Shadow?

"When shadow-work is neglected, the soul feels dry, brittle, like an empty vessel." ~ Steve Wolf, Therapist

The Shadow seeks to be known. It yearns to be understood.

Your Shadow is buried and locked in a jail cell deep within your unconscious. It will make you aware of its existence.

Both religion and modern spirituality focus on the "Love and Light."

This is an overemphasis on the feel-good elements of spiritual growth. This results in fear of the darker elements.

Spiritually bypassing your inner darkness results in a range of serious issues. These include pedophilia among priests and financial manipulation of followers among gurus. There is megalomania, narcissism, and God complexes among spiritual teachers.

"The purpose of learning to work with the unconscious is not just to resolve our conflicts or deal with our neuroses. We find there is a deep source of renewal, growth, strength, and wisdom. We connect with the source of our evolving character. We cooperate with the process whereby we bring the total self together. We learn to

tap that rich lode of energy and intelligence that waits within."
~ Robert A. Johnson, Author

Benefits of Shadow Work

- Shadow Work uncovers your core wounds, beliefs, traumas, and projections.
- Shadow Work can create clarity, understanding, harmony, and inner peace.
- Deep work makes changes in your Soul. This targets the very roots of our issues.
- Deeper love and acceptance of yourself.
- Better relationships with others, including your partner and children.
- Confidence to be your authentic self.
- Mental, emotional, and spiritual clarity.
- Enhanced creativity.
- Discovery of hidden gifts and talents.
- Deepened understanding of your passions and ultimate life purpose.
- Improved physical and mental health.
- It's important to remember that Shadow Work has no quick fixes. With persistence, benefits emerge, and your life is blessed.

Practice Shadow Work Daily.

Recommended Books:

Romancing the Shadow: A Guide to Soul Work for a Vital Authentic Self by Steve Wolf.

Mindful Shadow Work: Exercises For Befriending Your Dark Side, Healing Trauma, and Finding Joy by Aletheia Luna.

The Dark Side of the Light Chasers: Reclaiming Your Power by Debbie Ford.

Owning Your Own Shadow: Understanding the Dark Side of the Psyche by Robert A. Johnson.

22 - How to Enjoy Defining Moments, Critical Choices and Pivotal People

Each person has ten defining moments, seven critical choices, and five pivotal people who impact who they are. Defining moments, both positive and negative, are events that have changed or redefined who we are. ~ Stephen Covey, author of *The Seven Habits of Highly Effective People Defining Moments*

Life is full of choices and defining moments. Be honest with yourself in the moment of choice. This will help you stay on track. Then, live the life you want to live.

- Where has a defining moment changed your life?
- Did an illness or experience change your perspective?
- Did a career or relationship change?

Critical Choices

Bronnie Ware, author of *The Top Five Regrets of the Dying* states, there were five regrets that dying people told her about most often:

1. I wish I'd had the courage to live a life true to myself. Instead, I lived the life others expected of me.
2. I wish I hadn't worked so hard.
3. I wish I'd had the courage to express my feelings.
4. I wish I'd stayed in touch with my friends.
5. I wish I had let myself be happier.

Pivotal People

A pivotal person is someone who has had a positive or negative impact on a life. Pivotal people can be family members, friends, or acquaintances.

- **Supporter—** This is someone who believes in you and likes you.
- **Challenger—** A person who challenges you to achieve more.
- **Questioner—** This is a useful person to have on any team. They constructively ask tough questions.
- **Mentor or Coach—** Someone you can turn to for advice and guidance. Early on, this was a teacher or a parent.
- **Technical Expert—** You need a subject matter expert or technical guru in many situations.

Defining Moments

Everyone has defining moments. You define yourself by these moments. These include divorce, birth, illness, and death.

22 – How to Enjoy Defining Moments, Critical Choices and Pivotal People

"In every person's life, there have been defining moments, both positive and negative, that have defined and redefined who you are. Those events entered your consciousness with such power that they changed the very core of who and what you thought you were." ~ Dr. Phil McGraw, author and talk show host

Defining moments include divorce, birth, death, moving, and tragedy. They also include drugs, depression, affairs, and medical problems. Also, they can involve betrayal, near-death experiences, finances, etc.

My Defining Moments

- Brother Wayne was born when I was four years old.
- In grade three, my mother had to talk with a teacher.
- Grade twelve was selected to give the Valedictorian speech. Both parents acknowledged me after the speech.
- Deciding to go to college. At age eighteen left the farm to go to college.
- The first year of college.
- Deciding to get a business degree.
- Discovering psychology is my main interest.
- Deciding to live with my first girlfriend.
- Working in a group home with problem teens.
- Moving from Los Angeles to Toronto, Canada.
- Marrying my wife, Lyn.

- Moving to Sedona, Arizona.

Describing My Defining Moments

My Brother Wayne Born

My mother never told me she was going to have a baby. One day, she left for the hospital. When she came back, she had a baby in her arms.

That may be the reason I never felt connected to Wayne.

When I was ten, I convinced Wayne we should throw rocks at each other. So, out in the yard, sometimes a rock I threw would hit him.

Unconsciously, I felt anger toward him. Before he was born, I received all the attention from my mother. Afterward, I felt left on my own.

Grade Three Parent-Teacher Talk

Apparently, I had failing marks. I had no interest in school. After the meeting, my mother talked to me. I had no memory of what she said. However, I made a pivotal decision to apply myself to doing the schoolwork. Up to grade twelve, I always worked on studying all the time. Just before the final exams, my father remarked to my mother. I overheard it. *"That kid is going to go crazy with all the studying he is doing."* I passed my exams. So, I was able to attend college.

Grade Twelve Selected as Valedictorian

Stuart was the smartest in the class. Unknown to anyone, I used him as a model to compete against. He was a pivotal person.

Before the end of the term, the principal invited me into his office and said, *"Michael, you will be giving the Valedictorian speech."*

I was taken aback. The principal knew Stuart was coasting. Meanwhile, I worked very hard.

I spent a couple of weeks planning my speech while walking around the farm.

Valedictorian Speech

That evening, the mayor and influential community members gathered for dinner in a small room in our town. My mother and father also attended.

After dinner, I was asked to speak. For the first time I experienced an altered state of consciousness. I gave the speech without any awareness of doing so, and then I came back.

My parents and I drove home. When we got to our farmhouse, my parents sat me in a chair. They sat with me. I felt their love. It was a special moment when I had graduated into adulthood.

In the past, my father seldom spoke to me, except when he would tell me what work needed to be done. My mother always praised me.

Deciding to go to College

While in high school, I started thinking about how I could leave the farm. I just wanted out of all my father's fighting with my mother when he was drunk.

One day, I could go to college.

Most boy's fathers were farmers. They would stay and take over the family farm.

First, I thought I would be a geologist. I liked the outdoors and the rocks. Then, I decided I would be a journalist. I could travel the world and write.

First Year of College

I enrolled in the English Arts program.

I wanted to be a writer. I wrote an article for the college newspaper. The editor made changes, of course. I was devasted and decided I had no ability as a writer. It was a critical choice.

I finished out the year in the English program.

I used my mind to think about how to make money. I could study Law and become a lawyer. Then I would make a lot of money and do what I really enjoyed. By the way, I had no interest in Law.

I discovered that to enter Law first, I needed a three-year Business Degree to enter Law first. So, the next year, I enrolled in Business. Like Law, I had no interest in Business. It was only a means to an end. I could have been looking at what I would enjoy the most in life.

Next, I discover Psychology.

Discovering Psychology

Near the end of my Business Degree, I had a thought. What if I could study anything? What would I most enjoy?

I looked at my bookshelf, which was stacked three shelves high. It was all psychology books. I would love to study psychology.

In the fall, I enrolled in an after-degree psychology program. I studied all three years of psychology in one year.

It was the most enjoyable year of my life. It was a pivotal decision and a critical choice. I would call it a foundation stone, I celebrated for the rest of my life.

Decision Living with My First Girlfriend

I met this girl. We worked in different group homes for troubled teens. I felt a strong attraction to her.

She said she would only date me if I lived with her, but I ignored her concerns and moved into her apartment.

She had a three-year-old son, and I had no experience with children.

I worked for several days and nights straight at my job. When I came back to the apartment, the boy wanted to interact. I had no energy, and as I was exhausted, I retired to the bedroom to rest.

After a year's time, my girlfriend came to me and said she wanted a baby with me. I freaked out and told her, "NO."

She had refused to live with the father of her child. Now she wanted another child and to live with me.

I believe she wanted to reify the previous situation.

I lived with my girlfriend for three years. One day, when she was at work, I left. I took my clothes and moved to the YMCA.

My relationship was a defining moment. Up to that point, I had numbed my childhood feelings of trauma. Now I realized how shut down I was. I began the journey of feeling and healing my emotions.

Working with Troubled Teens

In Los Angeles, I worked in group homes with teen boys and girls for three years. In 1983, I became the Director of Chimo, the best-known group home.

I was inspired to check out group homes in Sedona, Arizona, again. This was thirty years later. I worked with teen girls up to age seventeen for about twelve years. This was a residential center for schooling and therapy. Every week, I also taught self-esteem and codependency recovery.

Then, I coached young girls and boys eighteen to twenty-eight for three years. These young adults needed help with anxiety, trauma, depression, and addictive behaviors.

I have dedicated my life to discovering and healing myself and others. This is emotionally, mentally, and spiritually.

Some teens have changed, and as adults, they live better lives now. I have also grown and transformed due of my interactions with the teens.

Moving from Los Angeles to Toronto and Marrying Lyn

In 1994, I moved from Los Angeles to Toronto. I had been invited to teach monthly hands-on Creation Energy Healing classes.

I lived with my girlfriend, Lyn. She was part of the initial group I taught in September 1993.

Once I channeled the Healing Energy, she recognized me right away. She went home and told her father she had met the man she would marry.

Lyn told me nothing. She waited to see if I would recognize her, and she was fine with that if I didn't.

When I taught in November, her father came to check me out. He was a strait-laced businessman. Of course, again, I knew nothing.

At the end of the November course, I hugged some students. Then I hugged Lyn.

In an altered state, I left my body, and I found myself out in the galaxy with stars all around. I had recognized Lyn. We married at the end of 1994.

My move to Toronto was a defining moment. Lyn and I transformed each other's lives in our thirty years together.

Moving to Sedona, Arizona

I first heard about Sedona while living in Los Angeles. I overheard someone say they had visited the Red Rocks of Sedona, Arizona, which piqued my interest.

In 1983, I returned each year to explore the hiking trails and make friends with the locals, in Sedona.

In 1995, I lived in Toronto with Lyn. One day, she said, "I hate my job and living in Toronto."

Without thinking, "I piped up I'd like to live in Sedona."

Lyn said, "Okay."

Lyn and I took a road trip. When Lyn first sighted the Red Rocks, tears welled up in her eyes. She felt she had come home.

We have lived in Sedona ever since. Our decision has proved pivotal, and we have both experienced many inner transformations over the years.

Sedona has powerful Earth energy (vortexes), which manifests as a polarity. Some people experience the positive aspect. You may experience feeling lighter in spirit or a sense of well-being.

Other people experience the other polarity. You may feel an emotional roller coaster of highs and lows, ungrounded, or imbalanced.

Writing Books

When I first moved to Sedona, I stopped teaching Energy Healing. Someone suggested I should write, but I never considered myself a writer.

I had a computer but no access to the Internet, so I got a few books on writing and started writing about my life. I wrote all day for five days and took the weekends off. After three years, I put that book aside. My wife told me no one would be interested in my story.

Then, I decided to write a fictional book. I thought people would be more interested. The title was *Questing the Emerald Heart*. It was about the search for the Holy Grail within ourselves.

Again, I wrote five days a week for two years. I then put the writing aside.

I needed to get a regular job making money to live. So, I worked in Sedona retail stores for five years.

In the beginning of 2010, I read in my astrology forecast that it would be a good year to write a book.

I returned to get the nonfiction book proofread. Also, I gathered stories from about twelve people on their experiences. I formatted the book and had it published on Amazon. The title is *Emotional Health: The Secret for Freedom from Drama, Trauma, and Pain.*

In 2012, I published again *Self-Esteem: A Teen's Guide for Girls.* This book was based on years of teaching teen girls in group homes.

In the beginning of 2024, I was inspired to write another book. My friends said, "Yes."

Writing has provided defining moments. It also shows my perseverance in creating a better life. Writing is also a critical choice in who I am and have become. I am an emotional and spiritual teacher in service to the world.

My life assists clients in accomplishing spiritual growth and higher consciousness.

Critical choices are those that have changed your life, positively or negatively. They act as major factors in determining who and what you become. Some examples of critical choices include friends, family, drugs, alcohol, school, college, jobs, and career, etc.

My Critical Choices

- Gave up drinking alcohol.
- At age twenty, I decided to live in Hawaii.
- At age thirty-three, I moved to Los Angeles from Alberta, Canada.
- Joined the Center for Feeling Therapy for three years.
- At age forty-two, I began teaching LaHo-Chi hands-on healing.
- Marrying my Twin Flame, Lyn.
- Studying with JJ Hurtak.
- Studying the Gene Keys.

Describing My Critical Choices

Gave Up Drinking Alcohol

Growing up, I had an alcoholic father.

I swore to myself never to drink alcohol.

When I lived in Hawaiʻi, I would go to a cocktail lounge. To relax after work, I would drink one or two black Russians.

During college breaks for two summers, I worked on a garbage truck. I went to the frat house and had one or two cold beers.

In college on weekends, I sat in my room, listened to music, and drank some Southern Comfort.

I used alcohol for relaxation. Otherwise, I was very uptight and controlled.

In college, I received initiation into Surat Shab Yoga meditation. It included repeating five mantras for two hours each day.

I practiced daily for ten years. After that, I had no desire for alcohol.

Decided to Live in Hawai'i

At age twenty, I decided to travel the world.

Most people liked Hawai'i. I chose to begin my travels in Hawaii on Oahu. I loved the sweet scent of flowers wafting through the warm air. I could have lived there for the rest of my life. However, after nine months, I returned to Alberta to attend college.

In Hawai'i, I learned to enjoy the beauty and sweetness of life. I also made enough money as a hotel attendant to pay for three college years.

Moved to Los Angeles, California

"Two roads diverged in the woods, and I took the one less traveled by. That had made all the difference." ~ Robert Frost, Poet

At thirty-three, I moved from Alberta, Canada, to Los Angeles. I had previously been at the Center for Feeling Therapy in L.A. Afterwards, I developed a strong intuitive sense of moving to L.A.

Fear arose that I would be destitute and homeless in L.A.

I trusted my intuition without question. It always has given me the choice of the "High Road."

In 1979, I moved to Los Angeles. I had a place to live and received a job as a printing salesman on the first day.

Center for Feeling Therapy

While in Edmonton, Alberta, I had a psychologist friend, Robert. One day, he said he had listened to a talk by two therapists from Los Angeles.

They offered a two-month training for people to attend. Then you could go back home and help others.

I was interested. So, Robert and I went to Los Angeles.

We had been there for a week. One night, Robert was in the living room of our apartment, and I was resting in the bedroom. Then Robert entered the bedroom and took his suitcases out of the closet.

I freaked out. After a few minutes, I got up. Robert wasn't in the living room. I went outside and didn't see any sign of him.

The next morning, our therapists told me Robert had left and had run away.

I decided to finish my two months at the Center. Then I went back to Edmonton.

Robert gave me the chance to experience the Center's training, which allowed me to make a critical choice. I soon returned to Los Angeles and spent three years at the Center.

My life shifted as I moved from numb to feeling emotions inside and healing.

Teaching LaHo-Chi Healing

In 1991, in Santa Monica, L.A., I asked my meditation teacher, "Is there a better way to heal." This is referred to as Energy Healing.

The teacher laid down and asked me to put my hands on four different parts of his body. Thus, I was initiated into Laho-Chi.

The Laho-Chi Master is Lao Tzu, a Chinese Master.

I started teaching monthly weekend classes to regular people and professionals. I taught in L.A. for three years and in Toronto for one year.

Laho-Chi eventually upgraded through me into a higher form of healing. I called it Creation Energy.

Creation Energy directly connects to Divine Source and Grace.

At age forty-six, I moved to Toronto, Canada, to teach this new form of healing: Creation Energy.

I now connect directly to the Divine and bring Divine Grace into a client's body.

I embraced my gift as an Energy Healer. To this day, I still have clients for Energy Healing.

Marrying My Twin Flame

A Twin Flame has a depth of connection. You both have a common purpose, working together for the good of humanity.

A Soul Mate is romantic. Soul Mates are karmic relationships. They stem from unresolved issues carried over from past lives. You have come together to learn about yourselves. Maybe you get the learning, or maybe not.

My Twin Flame, my wife Lyn, and I spent most of our thirty years working out our personal issues.

We have come together in the last four years to serve humanity and the world.

JJ Hurtak *Keys of Enoch*

The Keys of Enoch® contains sixty-four chapters of Spiritual-Scientific teaching. These are from two higher Teachers of universal intelligence "Enoch" and "Metatron."

Hurtak, in an out-of-body consciousness, directly experienced Enoch and Metatron face-to-face.

The Keys of Enoch® consist of teachings given on seven levels. They are read and visualized in preparation for the coming of the Brotherhood of Light.

The Hopi tribe in Arizona talks about the coming of Ultra-terrestrials, or Star Beings, returning to Earth. They will bring balance to the earth and reform society.

I have studied the Keys teachings since 1978.

I study in a group monthly. Sometimes, when Hurtak isn't traveling, he teaches directly in Sedona.

Beginning the study was a defining moment. It has also been a critical choice that raised my spiritual consciousness. Hurtak is also a pivotal person for me.

Gene Keys

"When you accept and begin dissolving your shadows, your suffering lessens. Also, your gifts and siddhis (flowering of gifts) start emerging. Embrace the Shadow, Release the Gift, Embody the Siddhi."~ Richard Rudd, author of *The Gene Keys*

There are sixty-four Shadow Subpersonalities. Eleven out of sixty-four shadow frequencies relate to you. These mental and emotional patterns arise out of your anger and fears. You encounter them through personal drama and relationship conflicts.

Richard Rudd, in his book *The Gene Keys*, explains the sixty-four victim/shadow patterns. On Rudd's website, you can receive a free profile. This identifies your specific eleven shadow patterns. You will also receive an introduction on how to begin reading your profile.

I began studying the Gene Keys about five years ago.

I learned in depth about my eleven victim patterns. I have struggled for most of my life with victim consciousness. When it arises occasionally, I recognize it and shift my awareness now.

The beauty of the Gene Keys is that I can move from a negative pattern to a gift of my talent Then, I can use that talent to assist a client. Some of my gifts have begun flowering with clients.

My life and my client's lives have developed more fully.

Richard Rudd is also a pivotal person for me.

A Pivotal Person is someone who has left an indelible impression on who you are and how you live. He or she may be a family member, friend, teacher, youth leader, counselor, co-worker, etc. Their influence can be either positive or negative.

My Pivotal People
- My Alcoholic Father.

- My Sweet Mother and Family.
- Kirpal Singh.
- Samuel.
- Hartha.
- My wife, Lyn.
- Mark Griffin.

Describing My Pivotal People

My Alcoholic Father

I would describe my father as a "lost soul." As an alcoholic, he disconnected from the family. He lost himself in the whiskey bottle almost daily.

He had no ambition or sense of direction. I always craved a connection with him. Never did I feel seen by my father. As an adult, I searched for mentors to fill my father's absence.

I took on my father's shame as my own.

As a teen, I never felt "good enough." Like my father, I felt disconnected. To survive in the family, I repressed all my feelings, including anger. In addition, I had no right to ask for what I needed.

Over my life, I have released the shame and anger of childhood. I no longer carry my father's energy within me. Rather than emptiness and pain, I feel peace. I have become stronger in my sense of who I Am.

My Sweet Mother and Family

22 – How to Enjoy Defining Moments, Critical Choices and Pivotal People

My mother was a workaholic, but also a sweet, kind-hearted person who always wanted the best for everyone.

My alcoholic father was missing in action. So, my mother took on running the farm and raising five kids.

My mother never had the time to sit down and talk with me. Because I never said anything, she thought I was okay. As a teen, I knew she loved me.

In my thirties, I visited my mother, two sisters, and youngest brother.

I had everyone sit down in the living room. Innocently, I explained how it had been for me growing up. It had been hell. I had never voiced anything before.

In the end, my mother remained silent. My brother was very upset. He commented on why I had to bring up the past. My oldest sister appreciated that, finally, someone had spoken up.

My mother is a pivotal person. I never realized how she kept all us kids safe, protected, and always wanted the best for us. I went to college because my mother took out a bank loan so I could attend my first year. College became a foundation stone for my spiritual growth.

Kirpal Singh

In college, I received initiation into Surat Shab Yoga meditation. It included repeating five mantras for two hours each day.

Two students of Kirpal Singh initiated me. I met Kirpal many years later.

Surat Shab Yoga opens the third eye to a vision of inner light and inner sound. The five mantras connect with the inner sound current.

I practiced this meditation daily for ten years. It gave me discipline. Although I never heard the sound current, I had many inner experiences. One time, I was out of body, seeing my physical body below me.

Meditation on the Divine Word is the spiritual base of all religions.

This meditation created a strong base for my Spiritual Growth.

Samuel

I have had a few best friends intermittently in my life. Most of them have been male.

Samuel was the longest, lasting about ten years.

One day, Samuel challenged me to stop being a garbage collector for the city. I could do better. At that time, I had college degrees. I worked for the city as it kept my mind free and allowed me to think about different things.

I took Samuel's challenge and began working in group homes for troubled teens.

Samual was a pivotal person in my transformation and interactions with the teens.

Hartha

Hartha is an African name meaning "treasure." She was truly a treasure to be valued.

She was a white woman in her sixties who lived in Toronto.

At the time when she contacted me, I lived in Los Angeles.

She had heard that I taught Energy Healing. Hartha wanted to learn what I taught. She had no previous experience. I would say her intuition guided her.

Hartha wanted to travel to Los Angeles for my next training. Her two adult daughters were dead set against it. She came anyway. She enjoyed the training. In the end, I gave all the students a book list so they could educate themselves further.

Hartha went back to Toronto to get some of the books. She found a "New Age" bookstore at the far end of Toronto. The owner was Joann.

When Joann touched the paper with the list of books, she felt my healing energy. She said to Hartha, "We need to get this guy up here to teach."

Hartha was pivotal in connecting me to Joann, and she was a treasure in that way.

I went to Toronto to teach and met my wife, Lyn.

Lyn

When Lyn and I work with clients, we serve as pivotal people for them.

Healing Testimonial

"Lyn and Michael create such a sacred and elevated space. Deep transfiguration takes place for those ready to dive deep into core issues. They create the best version of their true, authentic Selves.

"It's profoundly beautiful what can be accomplished. Michael and Lyn's unified fields join forces to create incredible healing experiences for clients.

"I highly recommend this dynamic duo. I have been working with them for many years now." Lori, Alchemist, Sedona, Arizona

Lyn and I also serve as pivotal people for each other.

I do Energy Healing for Lyn almost daily. She provides the same for me.

In the last four years, we have united in service to humanity and the world.

Mark Griffin

Mark was the owner of Sedona Mystical Tours. I stopped working for him at the beginning of 2020.

I learned how to assist clients on Sedona land journeys for many years.

Mark took a hands-off approach with me. I used my intuition to understand what clients needed, and then I provided a tailor-made tour.

Mark acted as a pivotal person as I learned to develop my own strengths and abilities.

My Review as a Tour Guide

"My family and I are deeply grateful for the healing experience we had with Michael. He was a very kind, empathetic guide and was very knowledgeable of the land. Through his guidance, he enabled us to connect with the flowering plants, herbs, and trees.

"His gentle and kind ways were very healing in itself. His energetic healing ministrations were well received by us and enabled especially my husband to transcend to higher awareness and spiritual connection.

22 – How to Enjoy Defining Moments, Critical Choices and Pivotal People

"A heartfelt thank you for the wonderful and enchanting vortex spiritual experience Michael!"

Sincerely, Jose, Celia, and Lauren, May 27, 2019

Summary Defining Moments, Critical Choices, and Pivotal People in Jacqueline's Life

Meeting the school children at age seven was a gift to Jacqueline. It was the first defining moment in her desire to explore the inherent beauty of the soul.

As a young adult, Jacqueline took a fork in the road when she attended University and studied biochemistry. This was a defining moment and also a critical choice.

Meditating at age eleven, the founder of Transcendental Meditation, Maharishi Mahesh Yogi, taught her how to meditate. This was another defining moment. Maharishi was a pivotal person.

At age thirty-three, she began a therapeutic model of growth and development and joined a spiritual order. This was another critical choice.

Jacqueline faced her fears. She Jacqueline transformed her thought processes from auto-pilot to piloting her thoughts and, therefore, her life's trajectory. These are more critical choices.

Dadi Janki and Jacqueline's mother and father were pivotal people in her life.

Suggestion:

Go through your life, write down, and contemplate your defining moments, critical choices, and pivotal people.

How have you been impacted?

What gifts and life skills have you developed?

You may have ten Defining Moments, seven Critical Choices, and five Pivotal People.

I had twelve Defining Moments, eight Critical Choices, and seven Pivotal People.

There can be more or less. I found it useful to understand a more in-depth view of my life.

"There is no passion to be found playing small. In settling for a life that is less than the one you are capable of living." ~ Nelson Mandela, South African Anti-Apartheid Activist, Politician, and First president of South Africa

Further Study:

The Seven Habits of Highly Effective People, by Stephen Covey.

Keys of Enoch, by JJ Hurtak.

The Gene Keys, by Richard Rudd.

Dr. Phil "Explores Defining Moments, Critical Choices, and Pivotal People," on YouTube.

23 - Benefits of Meditation: Unlocking Higher Consciousness

Meditation is a process of Self-discovery. All accomplished spiritual aspirants, yogis, and renunciates have acquired knowledge of the Absolute through meditation. ~ Sai Baba, Indian Guru

My wife, Lyn, and I have evolved three meditation practices for clients.

Meditation Align with the Divine/Absolute

First Mediation: Align with Your Still Point

- See, feel, imagine, or visualize a vertical Light ray throughout your spine.
- This Light comes from the Creator, Divine, God, or Source.
- Breathe directly from the Divine into the top crown of your head.
- Now, breathe it down into your energetic heart.

- Continue breathing down your body and into the earth below your feet.
- Finally, breathe all the way down into the central axis of the Earth.

Anything you do has a Still Point.

Still Point

"At the Still Point of the turning world ... Neither from nor towards. At the Still Point, there the dance is ... There is only the dance." ~ T.S. Eliot, Poet

In the Buddhist spiritual tradition, Four Still Points exist. The first is resistance or an obstacle.

Each Still Point Goes Deeper

1. The base of infinity of space.
2. The base of infinity of consciousness.
3. The base of the infinite consciousness.
4. The base of nothingness. This is nirvana: "no suffering; peace."

1. First, Still Point all the hindrances/resistances are stilled. These resistances include sensual desire, ill will, and sloth. Torpor, worry, and doubt are also included.

2. Second, Still Point to freedom from the three limitations of self-illusion, doubt, and attachment to rituals and rules.

3. Third Still Point the consciousness stretches and expands. It approaches a "black hole" of emptiness and nothingness. Consciousness fills the whole universe.

4. Nirvana, the ultimate still point, is realization.

There are several Still Points. Each is deeper and more "Still." Enjoy each stillness you experience.

Finding our inner Still Point requires paying attention to and feeling our inner world. This means recognizing and letting go of negative thoughts. You may want to free yourself from your constant chattering mind.

Your trauma from childhood creates negative thoughts. This is your left-overthinking brain.

Negative Mind Thinking

"The essence of trauma is disconnection from ourselves." ~ Gabor Mate, author of *In the Realm of Hungry Ghosts*

Balancing Negative Thinking (Left Brain)
- Negative thinking reversed.
- Sets boundaries protecting your well-being – Keeps you safe.
- Connects to your intuition.
- Uses inner wisdom to make decisions.
- Focused actions – Relaxation – Inner strength – Mental clarity.
- Connection to Divine/Higher Self – Inner power.

Second Meditation: Balance Negative Thinking Mind

- **Posture:** Sit straight in an easy cross-legged pose.
- **Mudra:** Make a cup of the two hands with both palms facing up, and the right hand resting on top of the left hand. Put this open cup at the level of the heart center. Relax elbows at the sides.
- **Eye Focus:** Your eyes are slightly open and looking down toward the hands.
- **Breath:** Inhale deeply with a long, steady stroke through the nose—Exhale in a focused stream through rounded lips. You will feel the breath go over your hands.
- **Mental Focus:** Let any thought or desire that is negatively distracting come into your mind. Breathe the thought and feeling in and exhale it out with the breath.

Michael: *I have been meditating since 1963.*

"Everything can be taken from a man but one thing. The last of the human freedom to choose one's attitude in any given set of circumstances, to choose one's own way." ~ Viktor Frankl, Psychiatrist, author of Search for Meaning

"The greatest discovery of any generation is that a human can alter his life by altering his attitude." ~ William James, an American philosopher and Psychologist

Third Meditation: Embrace Your Inner Body Sensations

- Now, bring attention to the inside of your body. What are the sensations: pleasure, discomfort, pain, tension?

Notice the strongest sensation? What draws your attention?

- Invite the sensation to have a voice. What do you imagine it would say? I am hungry, I am angry, I am sad, etc. Sit and stay with that feeling/sensation for at least 5 or 10 minutes.

- When thoughts arise, they return as silent observers and "feel/experience." Be one with the sensation. Imagine you embrace the sensation like a small child or a favorite pet.

- You cuddle and enjoy being at peace and present. with nothing You have nothing to do. No place you have to be. If thoughts arise, choose to put them aside.

Meditate daily.

Nine Types of Meditation Practice

1. Mindfulness meditation.
2. Spiritual meditation.
3. Focused meditation.
4. Movement meditation.
5. Mantra meditation.
6. Transcendental meditation.
7. Progressive relaxation.
8. Loving-kindness meditation.
9. Visualization meditation.

1. Mindfulness Meditation

"Feelings come and go like clouds in a windy sky. Conscious breathing is my anchor. Meditation is to be aware of what is going on. In your body. In your feelings. In your mind. In the world."
~ Thich Nhat Hanh, Buddhist Monk

Mindfulness meditation springs from Buddhist teachings. It is the most popular meditation in the West.

In mindfulness meditation, you pay attention to your thoughts. Observe them without judgment.

Concentrate and note any patterns.

Focus on your breath. Notice thoughts, feelings, and body sensations.

Use this meditation when you have no teacher to guide you. You can practice alone.

2. Spiritual Meditation

"You have to grow from inside out. None can teach you. None can make you spiritual. There is no other teacher but your own soul."
~ Marianne Williamson, Spiritual Teacher and Author

Spiritual meditation is practiced in most religions and spiritual traditions, including Christian, Sufi, and Jewish Kabbalist practices.

Many meditation methods are spiritual. Spiritual meditation focuses on developing a deeper understanding. Also, a better connection with your Higher Power.

Spiritual meditation can be practiced at home or in a place of worship.

3. Focused Meditation

"When meditation is mastered, the mind is unwavering like the flame of a candle in a windless place." ~ Bhagavad Gita

Focused meditation involves concentration using any of the five senses.

You can focus on something internal, like your breath. On the other hand, you can bring in external influences to focus your attention.

- Internal and External Examples
- Counting mala or prayer beads.
- Sound - listening to a gong.
- Focusing on a candle flame.
- Counting your breaths.
- Mantra repetition.

This practice may be difficult when you first begin.

If your mind wanders, simply come back to the meditation and refocus.

4. Movement Meditation

"Walk as if you are kissing the Earth with your feet." ~ Thich Nhat Hanh, Buddhist Monk

This is an active form of meditation in the present moment. Movement guides you into a deeper connection with your body.

Movement Meditation Includes:

Gardening—Working in the soil.

Labyrinth—It can be used as a tool to unwind your mind and to let go of stress or worries. Start at the beginning of a circular path. Continue to the center. At the center, send out a prayer if you like. Go back to the entrance.

Qi Gong—A system of coordinated body posture and movement, breathing, and meditation.

Tai Chi—Tai chi is a Chinese martial art. It is a series of deliberate, flowing motions, focused on deep, slow breaths.

Yoga—Combines physical postures, controlled breathing, and meditation.

Walking—Walking meditation has origins in Buddhism and is also a mindfulness practice. It may help you feel more grounded, balanced, and peaceful.

5. Mantra Meditation

"Meditation is a way for nourishing and blossoming the divinity within you. Life is not always perfect. Like a road, it has many bends, ups and downs, but that's its beauty." ~ Amit Ray, Indian Author and Spiritual Master

Two Types of Mantra Meditation, Japa and Kirtan

Japa is a quiet and personal meditation. You chant with prayer beads.

Kirtan, on the other hand, is a joyous group meditation. It is a call-and-response style with musical instruments.

Mantra practice has Buddhist and Hindu roots. This method exists within spiritual traditions, including Christianity and Shamanism.

23 – Benefits of Meditation: Unlocking Higher Consciousness

Most mantra meditation techniques have two essential components. These are mindfulness meditation and mantra recitation or chanting.

Mantras can be spoken, chanted, whispered, or repeated in your mind. This can be out loud or quietly.

Some people enjoy mantra meditation because they find it easier. They focus on a word rather than on their breath. Others enjoy feeling the vibration of the sound in their body.

After chanting the mantra for some time, you'll be more alert and in tune, allowing you to experience deeper levels of awareness.

This is also a good practice for people who prefer sound rather than silence. A common word is "OM."

If the chosen mantra has a deeply personal or spiritual meaning to you, it can even act as a touchpoint or spiritual anchor to assist you in your meditation.

For two-thirds of my life, I have used many mantras. These include OM, the Gayatri Mantra, Om Mani Padme Hum, Ehyeh Ehyeh Asher, and Ho'oponopono.

OM: One of the most popular chanting mantras in yoga. It's the sound of the universe.

Gayatri Mantra: "On the absolute reality and its planes, on that finest spiritual light, meditate, as remover of obstacles, that it may inspire and enlighten us."

Om Mani Padme Hum: Hail the Jewel in the Lotus.

Tibetan Buddhists use it to achieve the ultimate state of compassion.

Ehyeh Ehyeh Asher: I AM that I AM.

Ho'oponopono: It is an ancient Hawaiian Mantra. The meaning is, "I'm sorry. Please forgive me. Thank you. I love you."

6. Transcendental Meditation - TM

"Transcendental Meditation is the technique that leads to unity consciousness." ~ Maharishi Yogi, Creator Transcendental Meditation

In the 1960s, Maharishi gained global recognition when he taught TM to the Beatles.

There is a difference between Transcendental Meditation, TM, and other forms of meditation.

In TM, the mantra is a sound used to help your mind settle down. It is a silent mantra meditation.

In TM, the purpose is to reach a state of peace or pure consciousness. This is a state of inner peace, clarity, and connectedness.

TM is a kind of meditation that involves effortlessly and silently saying a specific mantra until you transcend conscious thought.

You keep repeating the mantra over and over. Your mind gradually settles into subtle levels, and you eventually transcend the mantra and consciousness.

TM has a frequency like OM. This is primordial hum.

You are given a mantra that is unique to you. It is based on the instructor's knowledge of you. Also, it is what will work best for you.

TM was the first meditation I practiced. It worked beautifully for six months, but then I no longer transcended consciousness during meditation.

It was time for a different meditation. I went from no effort to maximum concentration.

With Surat Shab Yoga, I repeated five mantras for two hours each day.

I practiced this meditation daily for ten years.

7. Progressive Relaxation

"An anxious mind cannot exist in a relaxed body. It might be naive to say we think with our muscles. But it would be inaccurate to say we think without them. There is probably no more general remedy than rest." ~ Edmund Jacobson. He is a U.S., trained physician who noticed that all his patients with illness showed chronic muscle tension. He theorized that if muscle tension was significantly decreased, the chance of illness would diminish.

The body's muscles respond to thoughts of perceived threat with tension or contraction.

Muscular tension is the most common symptom of stress. It can lead to stiffness, pain, and discomfort. Also, distorted and misaligned posture and joint stability can manifest.

Relaxation techniques were designed to relax muscles. If you relieve tension in the body, the mind will follow. Sometimes, we are too stressed to slow our minds down first.

As the body relaxes, so does the mind.

Jacobson found he could quiet the mind by reversing the brain-muscle process. When muscles relax, the brain responds by quieting.

8. Loving-Kindness Meditation

"Just as a mother would protect her only child with her life, even so, let one cultivate a boundless love towards all beings."
~ Buddha

Loving Kindness Meditation, or Metta meditation, is a centuries-old Buddhist practice.

It involves repeating a set of phrases. You send out prayers that you and all beings be happy.

With your eyes closed and your back straight, focus your attention on your heart. If it helps, place your hand on your heart.

First, send yourself loving-kindness by repeating your chosen phrases three times.

"May I/you be healthy, well, light, happy, and peaceful?"

Now imagine you and some of your friends sitting in a circle.

Repeat your chosen phrase three times.

"May you be healthy, safe, and strong."

Next, imagine the loving-kindness spreading out from your small circle to the neighborhood. Then, see it spreading from your country, continent, and worldwide to all life forms.

Repeat your chosen phrase three times.

"May all beings on Earth be healthy, safe, and strong."

Next, imagine loving-kindness radiating from the Earth into space. It touches all life forms in the cosmos.

Repeat your chosen phrase three times.

"May all beings throughout all time and space be healthy, safe, and strong."

Slowly bring your awareness back to your breath and your surroundings. Then, gradually open your eyes.

9. Visualization Meditation

"Proper visualization by the exercise of concentration and will-power enables us to materialize thoughts. Not only as dreams or visions in the mental realm but also as experiences in the material realm." ~ Yogananda

Visualization meditation focuses on enhancing feelings of relaxation, peace, and calmness. This occurs by visualizing positive scenes, images, or figures.

Imagine a scene vividly using all five senses. Add as much detail as possible. It can also involve holding a beloved or honored figure in mind. Your intention is to embody their qualities.

Another form of visualization meditation involves imagining yourself succeeding at specific goals. This increases focus and motivation.

Many people use this meditation to boost their mood, reduce stress levels, and promote inner peace.

Michael: *I have meditated for over fifty years. I began with Transcendental Meditation. Then I practiced Surat Shab Yoga mantras for ten years, two hours a day. I have practiced*

Mindfulness, Spiritual, and Focused meditations. Movement meditation involved yoga, labyrinths, medicine wheels, and hiking in nature.

It is suggested that the mediators start with short periods of 10 minutes or so. As you practice daily, it becomes easier. Keep your attention focused on breathing.

"Sit consistently for 20 minutes a day. Do this for 100 days straight. Couple that with an additional 2 to 5 minutes of meditation throughout the day. This breaks up the chaos. You will soon be feeling the benefits." ~ Pedram Shojai, Former Taoist Monk

Recommended Books:

The Art of Stopping Time: Practical Mindfulness for Busy People by Pedram Shojai.

Maharishi Mahesh Yogi - A Living Saint for the New Millennium by Theresa Olson.

24 - Spiritual Growth: How to Be in Higher Consciousness

Our normal waking consciousness, rational consciousness as we call it, is but one special type of consciousness. Whilst all about it...there lie potential forms of consciousness entirely different.
~ William James

Overview of Levels of Consciousness

Many levels of consciousness exist. Freud defined the unconscious, subconscious, and conscious.

Hindu Upanishads have four levels, with the last level being enlightenment.

Richard Barrett's model has seven levels, the last of which is service consciousness. It is inspired by Maslow's Hierarchy of Needs and identifies seven levels of higher consciousness, ranging from survival to service consciousness. The model has been tested for over two decades. Richard Barrett is an author and coach.

An eighth level is full-spectrum consciousness. At the eighth level, you have mastered all levels.

I first describe Barrett's seven levels and add full-spectrum consciousness. Then, I explain Michael Beckwith and Mary O'Malley's models.

You operate at a consciousness level, depending on the stage of development you have reached.

What happens if a situation triggers your survival, safety, or security?

You immediately drop down to one of the first three levels of consciousness.

Barrett's Seven Levels of Consciousness

Level 1: Survival Consciousness

"Pain is physical; suffering is mental. Beyond the mind, there is no suffering. Pain is essential for the survival of the body, but none compels you to suffer. Suffering is due entirely to clinging or resisting. It is a sign of our unwillingness to move on, to flow with life." ~ Nisargadatta Maharaj, Spiritual Teacher, Advaita Non-Duality

The first level of personal consciousness is all about survival. To survive, you need clean air, water, and wholesome food. You need to feel financially secure.

Were your survival needs unmet as a child? Then, as an adult, you will have little trust in others to take care of your needs. You will be stressed and want to control.

Michael: *My mother looked after the family's needs for food and shelter. We never went hungry. However, I suffered because I resisted the flow of life. As a child, my emotional needs were never*

met. Thus, my inner child felt unsafe and wanted to control everything. I learned to flow with life decades later.

Level 2: Relationship Consciousness: Conforming

"If I accept the fact that my relationships are here to make me conscious instead of happy. Then my relationships become a wonderful self-mastery tool that keeps realigning me with my higher purpose for living." ~ Eckhart Tolle, *The Power of Now*

The second level is about feeling safe, loved, protected, and belonging. If your needs were unmet as a child, you would want to be liked as an adult and be anxious. On the other hand, if you were loved and protected, you could take care of your needs and relationships.

In conscious relationships, your needs get fulfilled. Also, your loved one's needs are satisfied.

Each of you takes personal responsibility and communicates authentically. You stay present with each other.

Michael: *Most of my life I remained unconscious in my relationships. Growing up, I never received kudos from my father. My inner child always wanted people to like him. He wanted people to tell him what a good job he had done. I spent the last thirty years mastering my relationship with my wife. Now I have moved into higher consciousness in relationships.*

Level 3: Differentiating Consciousness: Self-Esteem

"Every morning, look in the mirror. You are beautiful and wonderful." ~ Lailah Gifty Akita, author of *Pearls of Wisdom*

The third level of personal consciousness is about feeling secure and your level of esteem.

When you feel "unworthy/less than," trauma from childhood and teen years gets triggered. You may feel anxious and upset.

Were you recognized for your better qualities as a teenager? Did you have good relationships with your parents, peers, and authority figures? Then you will have good self-esteem. You feel confident.

Michael: *I picked up feeling unworthy of my father. However, I always thought it was my own. I see my alcoholic father as "a lost soul." He had no direction or motivation. As a teen, I suffered from low self-esteem. This drove me throughout my life to improve my life. In my fifties, I taught weekly self-esteem recovery classes to groups of teens.*

Level 4: Transformation Consciousness: Individuating

"I have a dream that one day, this nation will rise up and live out the true meaning of its creed. "We hold these truths to be self-evident, that all men are created equal." ~ Martin Luther King

The fourth level of consciousness is finding freedom and autonomy. It is claiming your right to be in charge of your life. This is called sovereignty or your right to "BE."

You ask questions such as, "Who AM I?" and "What is Important?"

You fully express yourself without fear of what others may think or say. Choices are made in alignment with your sovereignty.

Now, you remove your ego mask and march to your tune.

Historical examples are the Dali Lama, Einstein, John F. Kennedy, Martin Luther King, Mother Teresa, and Nelson Mandela.

Michael: *In my thirties, I wore an "ego mask." I so numbed my face that people called me "stone face." At the Center for Feeling Therapy in Los Angeles, I began exploring my feelings through therapy. Over three years, I began discovering my inner nature. Today, I am a sovereign being. I am the King and ruler of my life.*

Level 5: Internal Cohesion Consciousness: Self-Actualizing

They master internal cohesion consciousness when they uncover their sense of purpose or personal, transcendent meaning for existence.

"They master making a difference consciousness by actualizing their sense of meaning by collaborating with others to positively contribute to the world." ~ Richard Barrett, author

The fifth level of human consciousness is about finding meaning in life and creating a vision for the future.

You question, "Why am I in this body?" Also, you ask, "How can I fully express myself?"

This can be a daunting inquiry for those who lack a sense of purpose. Your purpose will be obvious to others who are gifted with a particular talent.

If you are unsure of your purpose, simply focus on what you love to do and pay attention to what is immediately in front of you.

Follow your joy. Develop your most obvious talents and pursue your passion.

Your purpose may feel small or large, but it is what your soul came to do. Commit your energy to your soul's purpose, and unexpected events will occur to support you.

Michael: *I struggled for sixty percent of my life questioning my life purpose. Constantly, I banged my head against a stone wall. Frustration dogged my every step. Unknown to me my purpose unfolded with each step. Now I have many talents. The upliftment of humanity's consciousness through Energy Healing is my wife's and my soul's purpose.*

Level 6: Making a Difference Consciousness

"Do not waste what remains of your life in speculating about your neighbors unless with a view to some mutual benefit. To wonder what so-and-so is doing and why, or what he is saying, or thinking, or scheming. In a word, anything that distracts you from fidelity to the ruler within you. This means a loss of opportunity for some other task." ~ Marcus Aurelius, Roman Emperor, and Stoic Philosopher, author of *The Meditations*

The sixth level of human consciousness is about making a difference in the world, whether in your family, workplace, community, nation, or global society.

Actualize your sense of purpose by cooperating with others for mutual benefit and fulfillment.

If you are a leader, you realize fulfilling your purpose is strongly conditioned by connecting with others. Facilitate the work of those who support you.

Enlightened leaders understand it is through their followers that they impact the world.

24 – Spiritual Growth: How to Be in Higher Consciousness

The more easily you connect and empathize with others, the easier it is to fulfill your destiny.

Connect with others in unconditional loving relationships.

Most Enlightened Leaders are unknown to the public. Some known ones are Buddha, Jesus, Krishna, Mother Mary, Sai Baba, and Yogananda.

Michael: *I had no idea I could make a difference when I was young. However, I was curious and desired to travel and explore the world. As a lone wolf, I believed I had to do everything myself. Although, when the occasion arose, I could work with others. Nowadays, I strongly desire to cooperate in synarchy/jointly with groups.*

Level 7: Service Consciousness: Service

"Everyone can be great because everyone can serve. This country will not be a good place for any of us to live in unless we make it a good place for all of us to live in. I have found that among its other benefits, giving liberates the soul of the giver." ~ Martin Luther King, Jr.

The seventh level of human consciousness is about selfless service. This is the cause or the work which allows you to use your talents. The work you were born to do.

You reach this level of consciousness when making a difference becomes a way of life.

When you surrender to your soul, you now fully live the life of a soul-infused personality. Also, you are at ease with uncertainty and embrace whatever opportunities come your way.

At this stage, you find yourself needing time for quiet and reflection. You receive inspiration from your soul. So, you live and breathe your purpose every moment of life.

You will never retire. What you previously considered work now becomes play. At this level, you let the doing flow through "Being."

Devote your life to selfless service in pursuit of your passion, purpose, and your vision.

Michael: *Over my life, I have learned to surrender my personality to my soul and the Divine. I now recognize selfless service and dedicate my talents to it.*

Full-Spectrum Consciousness

"A full-spectrum approach to human consciousness and behavior means that men and women have a spectrum of knowing available to them. A spectrum that includes, at the very least, the eye of flesh, the eye of mind, and the eye of spirit." ~ Kenneth Wilber, American Theorist and Writer of Transpersonal Psychology

You may have mastered every stage of your ego needs and soul desires when you reach your latter years.

When you operate from Full-Spectrum Consciousness, you respond appropriately to all situations. You respond with inner calm, without fear, upset, or anxiety. People operating from Full-Spectrum Consciousness display the following attributes:

By staying healthy, you master your "survival" needs. You also look after your body and financial security, protecting yourself from harm and injury.

Building friendships allows you to master "relationship" needs. Furthermore, it creates family connections that feel like love and belonging.

You master your "self-esteem" needs by building a strong sense of self-worth. Also, you act responsibly in everything you do.

You master your "transformation" by having the courage to embrace your authentic self. Furthermore, you overcome the fears of deficiency needs.

- You master "internal cohesion" needs by embracing your soul's purpose. Creativity is expressed.

- You master making a difference by actualizing your sense of "purpose." Furthermore, you connect with others in unconditional loving relationships.

- You devote your life to your purpose. Moreover, you make a "lasting contribution" to the well-being of humanity, the planet, and future generations.

I now describe Michael Beckwith's stages of Spiritual Growth.

Michael Beckwith 4 Stages Spiritual Growth

"Your life is a journey from unconsciousness to higher consciousness." ~ Michael Beckwith, Minister at Agape Church in Los Angeles

1. **To Me: Victim Consciousness:** At the mercy of circumstances.

   Reacting, resisting, judging. No control. Fear. Positive growth happens when you let go of blame. This results in taking personal responsibility. A catalyst to this growth is either pain or insight.

2. **By Me: Manifestation Consciousness:** Realize blame is giving power away. Empowerment, take responsibility. I am in control. I can do this. Determination. Personal ownership.

   You understand your life role and ability to influence, attract, and manifest. Positive growth occurs when you let go of control.

3. **Channeling Consciousness:** Grace and flow. Life is giving. Humility. No control or need for it. Connected.

   "You find yourself having more and more insights. Having revelations. Having a level of wisdom and guidance and direction. It's not coming from figuring something out. More intuition is being activated. There's an allowing state. You become a vehicle for something to occur." ~ Michael Beckwith

4. **As Me: Being Consciousness:** I am universal awareness; Source, Spirit, God—a unique expression of that. No separation. Oneness: Peace, Joy, Love.

You feel a sense of "at Onement."

You feel your divinity and connectedness with God and with everyone. Your life is an expression of God.

Where do you see yourself now according to these four evolutionary stages of consciousness?

Michael: *In Beckwith's stages of consciousness, I never blamed others. My adult rules my life rather than my inner child. When the inner child wants to rule, I calm him. My intuition has been developed since my teens. I have cultivated my connection with the Divine and Divine Grace.*

Next, I will describe Mary O'Malley's Six Phases of Higher Consciousness. She added two more to Michael Beckwith's four.

Mary added, *"Life happens in you."* And *"Life happens for you,"* and called them the "Six Phases of Higher Consciousness."

Mary O'Malley is an author, counselor, and leader in the field of awakening.

"Thank you, Mary, for your contribution to the evolution of human consciousness." ~ Eckhart Tolle, author of *The Power of Now*

Six Phases of Higher Consciousness

"Higher consciousness is a state of elevated awareness and perception in which a person has a deeper understanding of the nature of reality, the self, and various spiritual aspects of life. These play an important role in one's personal evolution and psychological development." ~ Mary O'Malley

As you move through each of the outlined levels, you will make major leaps and bounds towards enlightenment.

Take a few minutes to explore each level of consciousness.

As you read, I invite you to keep checking in with yourself. You are being given important information.

Remember that the most powerful thing you can do for your healing is to combine your attention and your experience, no matter what it brings up for you.

In the first two phases, you resist and want to control Life. You are unable to open to Life. There is no showing up in the creative river of Life.

In the next two phases, you become curious. You become interested in what you experience in each moment. The more you experience, the easier and more difficult it becomes. Life knows what it is doing.

The final two phases are about coming home. You live the truth that Life is for you. The more you relax into the flow. Joy of Life moves through you. You are Life.

"You are not in the universe. You are the universe. An intrinsic part of it." ~ Mary O'Malley

Most people live in the first two phases of higher consciousness, to and by you.

In the middle of these is a doorway into the last four. Life is waking you up from the contraction of the first two. Then, you open into the last four. This is for your healing, for the healing of all beings, and for you to become a healing presence in the world.

Human beings are evolving from the first level of consciousness to the sixth. Most days, you will experience a number of these phases. They are all part of Life. As you evolve, you will recognize and embrace them all.

24 – Spiritual Growth: How to Be in Higher Consciousness

1st Phase of Higher Consciousness: Life Happens To You

"When you are just EXISTING, life happens to you… and you manage; when you are truly LIVING, you happen to live… and you lead." ~ Steve Maraboli, author

You have probably lived most of your life feeling that Life is happening to you. You never know what will happen next.

Every day, you get a little older. Death is always lurking around the corner.

The more unconscious you are, the more you feel like a victim. You see Life as a threat.

You stay caught in your head. So, you resist, react, and explain.

You hope to figure everything out.

Open to Life, right here, right now.

2nd Level of Higher Consciousness: Life Happens By You

"You cannot control what happens to you. However, you can control your attitude toward what happens to you. In that, you will master change rather than allowing it to master you." ~ Brian Tracy, author

"Healing is a different type of pain. It's the pain of becoming aware of the power of one's strengths and weakness. Of one's capacity to love or do damage to oneself and to others. Of how the most challenging person to control in life is ultimately yourself." ~ Caroline Myss, author

You believe you can control life rather than being a victim. This level of consciousness can give you a great feeling of personal power.

Moving out of the victimhood of the first stage of higher consciousness is necessary.

Eventually, you evolve into setting intentions. With intentions, you work with feeling what you want to generate. Opening into Life brings you what you most deeply long for

There is a relatively new form of control in which you believe you can control your reality. Your mind tells you all you must do is think the right thoughts. The main difficulty with this is that it never works.

To stay caught in this phase of higher consciousness is to be cut off from the creative flow of Life. Instead, show up for Life.

3rd Level of Higher Consciousness: Life Happens In You

"We don't see things as they are. We see them as we are." ~ Anais Nin, a French author

You begin getting an inkling that Life is something to be listened to and opened to. You start evolving into the next phase, where Life is happening in you.

At this phase, you begin realizing something very startling. Most of the time, rather than experiencing Life, you think about it.

When you experience Life through your thoughts, you stop experiencing it as it is. When was the last time you truly saw a loved one's face?

In this phase, you realize that your suffering never comes from your life experiences. Instead, it comes from your stories about what is happening. It comes from inside of you!

This is where you begin to live the "you-turn." You realize healing comes when you turn your attention within.

4th Level of Higher Consciousness: Life Happens For You

"You stop trying to forcibly manage the thoughts, beliefs, and actions that arise from your mind. You ask to be guided by a source greater than yourself. You find a world of support showing up in surprising ways." ~ Debbie Ford, author

You become curious about what is happening rather than reacting and controlling. Then, realize your life is for you. You are one step further on your journey.

Life is never a random series of events. It is a highly intelligent unfolding that puts you in the exact situations you need. Life knows what it is doing.

You begin showing up for Life exactly as it is. Yes, the flow of Life includes pain, loss, and death. Resisting the pains of Life only turns them into suffering.

Directly experience your pain. Bring your attention to your experience, whatever it is. Sense it, feel it in your body.

When you respond rather than react, what is bound up loosen. That trapped energy flows freely, bringing the bliss of openness.

Remember, Life is set up to bring up what has been bound up. Open up. Show up for Life!

Close your eyes for a few moments. Open into this living moment of your life.

Sense it, feel it. This is the only moment that matters in your whole life. It is the moment where Life is happening!

5th Level of Higher Consciousness: Life Happens Through You

"You find your way by being sensitively and sensually connected to exactly where you are. Letting 'here' reach out and lead you."
~ Cynthia Bourgeault, author

This phase shows you that there is no such thing as an ordinary moment. Life is speaking to you at all moments.

Becoming curious about what you experience. Give it the light of compassionate attention. Allow Life to move through you.

Recognize that Life is trustworthy. It may not always be likable, but it knows what it is doing.

Trust Life. Every morning, you wake up with a sense of adventure. Your belly is soft, and your mind is curious. Also, your heart is open.

Open to Life even when you face deep challenges. If you react, give it the attention it needs to let go.

The vibrant flow of Life moves freely through you, bringing creativity and joy. You experience deep gratitude for everything.

Everything that has happened to you, even the difficult, has been a journey back into Life.

Step by step, Life allows you to be fully here for Life.

6th Level of Higher Consciousness: Life Is You

24 – Spiritual Growth: How to Be in Higher Consciousness

"You are not in the universe; you are the universe, an intrinsic part of it. Ultimately, you are not a person. You are a focal point where the universe is becoming conscious of itself. What an amazing miracle." ~ Eckhart Tolle, *The Power of Now*

You are no longer a separate being. Instead, you merge completely back into the creative flow of Life. Understand that everything: every rock, person, cloud, molecule, and ladybug is you. You are Life!

Jacqueline's Spiritual Growth: Becoming Conscious

Jacqueline's journey began at age seven. She describes her challenges and the positive choices she made.

Jacqueline: *My spiritual self-growth came at an early age. I believe that a defining moment was when I was seven years old. Rakhikol, India, is not a place I can easily forget. I was visiting this isolated village in the hilly jungle of central India.*

My father had a coal mine there, which was manned by the local villagers. Dad had organized the building of a little schoolhouse with the mine manager, a Scottish chap named David Wightman, who lived in a bungalow on the property with his wife Jennie and a rather cheeky parakeet.

One afternoon, my mother took me to meet the children at the school. My function was to greet each child and to pass out hard candy. They were dressed in their best attire, and most of them were barefoot. Each child displayed gratitude for such a little offering. I remember being deeply moved by their generosity of spirit, their smiles and giggles of delight and deep bows while saying, "Namaste," roughly translated, "The Spirit in me meets the same Spirit in you." It was a poignant moment for me. Although these children were poor, their souls were the antithesis of poverty. The experience was a gift to me and the first defining moment in my desire to explore the inherent beauty of the soul.

As a young adult, I was still fascinated with my spiritual quest. (Living in India and having a Zoroastrian father grounded me in both the spiritual and linear). I took a "fork in the road" when I attended University and studied biochemistry. The sciences have always fascinated me, but I believe in hindsight that it was important for me to impress my father and demonstrate to him that I could do anything my five brothers could. It was clear to me that he valued the sciences, and my worth was calibrated by what I did. I have always been very spiritual. I started meditating at age eleven when the founder of Transcendental Meditation, Maharishi Mahesh Yogi, taught me how to meditate.

Emotional maturity is linked to spiritual flourishing. Some of my childhood experiences were toxic and did not contribute to my emotional well-being. At age thirty, I began a "therapeutic model of growth" and development and joined a spiritual order to enhance my well-being. We come out of our family of origin on auto-pilot and are doomed to function from that place of disjunction unless we look at the thoughts and assumptions that drive our lives. I had many setbacks as I delved into the arch of my emotional autopilot. Many issues surfaced that challenged me, but as I faced my fears, I transformed my thought process from autopilot to piloting my thoughts and, therefore, my life's trajectory.

I have always longed to know God. It wasn't until I met Dadi Janki of the Brahma Kumaris, who challenged my assumptions and patiently answered my queries, that I had a close encounter with the Divine.

In hindsight, I believe what was helpful to me was coming from an Indian culture where spirituality is inherent in the framework of everyday life. What I wish I had known earlier was that one can cultivate a direct relationship with God.

Books for Further Study:

A New Psychology of Human Well-Being, by Richard Barrett.

What's in the Way is the Way, by Mary O'Malley.

The Manifestation Book 4 of 6, by Blair Abee.

Mystical Hope, by Cynthia Bourgeault.

25 - Service Consciousness: How to Live in the Present Moment

Finding your soul purpose and living it out is the greatest gift you can give yourself. Choosing to follow your passion floods your life with meaning...Your work becomes your mission. ~ Richard Barrett, Author

The seventh level of human consciousness is about selfless service. It is the work that allows you to use your gifts and talents. This is the work you were born to do.

You reach this level of consciousness when making a difference becomes a way of life. You surrender to your soul.

The person with the deepest consciousness and compassion has a responsibility to help things go well.

Deeper consciousness generates clearer vision and more mature moral clarity.

"The way to freedom is through service to others. The way to happiness is through meditation and being in tune with God...break the barriers of your ego, shed selfishness, free yourself from the consciousness of the body, forget yourself, do away with

this prison house of incarnations, melt your heart in all, be one with creation." ~ Yogananda

"The more you try to force life to flow where you would like it to go. As opposed to where it wants to go. The less efficient you become and, the more energy you use." ~ Richard Rudd, *The Gene Keys*

I describe Spirituality as four levels of consciousness/higher awareness. Other ways and other names may be used to describe the levels.

God Consciousness: No separation exists between you and the Divine. You are one and the same.

Michael: *I connect with the Divine daily*

Transcendental Consciousness: You silence all your senses while completely conscious.

Michael: *This occurs on occasion for me.*

Unity Consciousness: You sense a deep connection with all life.

Michael: *I sense this when I go out on the land in Sedona, Arizona.*

Cosmic Consciousness: Cosmic Consciousness involves inner awareness beyond the everyday world.

Michael: *I have a strong intuitive Inner Knowing. I can access this at any time.*

Service Consciousness: Service consciousness is when you no longer identify only with your body. You also identify

25 – Service Consciousness: How to Live in the Present Moment

with emotions and thoughts. You realize a spark of the Divine is your True Being.

"I now describe my experience with various spiritual teachers. They all are in Service Consciousness. I have met and studied with some. Others, I have studied their teachings." ~ Richard Rudd, author and Mystical Poet, Teacher

"You may experience helping others as a gift to them. It also comes back as a gift to you in some way. It is prosperity for all. Lack no longer exists. Here in lies the True nature of Service." ~ Richard Rudd

Richard Rudd's inner journey began early in life. He experienced strange energies rushing throughout his body, culminating in a major spiritual experience at the age of twenty-nine.

He emerged from what he calls "a field of limitless light." This lasted three days and three nights.

Richard was entrusted with a sacred teaching of the wisdom of *The Gene Keys*. *The Gene Keys* integrates your shadows (trauma), gifts (higher frequencies), and siddhis (developed gifts).

Michael: *I have studied the Gene Keys in depth since January 2021.*

"Serving the Truth becomes your life instead of just an isolated event. It removes the abstractness from spirituality. That's the opportunity of real spirituality to be in service." ~ Adyashanti, author of *Falling into Grace*

"Silence is not merely a state but an essence that is the background of all states and all things." ~ Adyashanti

Silence is alignment with the Divine. It moves through your whole body into the Earth and brings peace and silence.

Silence is the essence of all states of Higher Consciousness.

How long can you stay in a state of silence?

Michael: *I studied Adyashasti's teachings.*

Eckhart Tolle *The Power of Now*, Self-Help Author, Spiritual Teacher

"Accept - then act. Whatever the present moment contains, accept it as if you had chosen it. Always work with it, not against it. Make it your friend and ally, not your enemy. Realize deeply that the present moment is all you ever have. Make the Now the primary focus of your life. It is through the mistakes that the greatest learning happens on an inner level." ~ Eckhart Tolle

Tolle embodies the power of Presence. He resides in an awakened state of consciousness twenty-four hours a day. It transcends ego and left-brain mind chatter. Tolle sees this consciousness as the next step in human evolution.

Michael: *I studied Tolle for years.*

J.J. Hurtak Author, Spiritual Teacher

"The holy eyes of our fathers from consciousness beginning to watch the formation of the "brotherhoods of light. The brotherhoods bring the message of 'peace and preparation.' from the firmament. The brotherhoods receive the whole light beings" who come in the appearance of man with quanta mechanical corpuscles of light and 'move in the midst of man' by gravitational flux line controls so that they who will see 'will see.' The brotherhoods come and return in a "flash of light." Keys of Enoch. Key 316.

The *Keys of Enoch* contain spiritual-scientific teaching from two higher teachers. These teachers of universal intelligence are "Enoch" and "Metatron."

In 1973, Enoch "lifted up" Hurtak in a body of Light.

Over two days, Enoch "downloaded" 64 keys into Hurtak. These revelations were the *Keys of Enoch*.

Enoch answered a prayerful plea from Hurtak. The prayer explained the purpose of life on Earth. New generations will be recorded for future transformations of the race.

Enoch "initiates into Light." He is the same Enoch of the Bible. Enoch took Hurtak further to Metatron, a visible manifestation of the Divine.

The Academy for Future Science is an international non-governmental organization. It works to bring cooperation between science and spirituality. This is through the positive use of consciousness. The Keys of Enoch brings a greater unity between scientific and spiritual pathways. These link human evolution with Higher Evolution. They connect humankind with the greater Master Plan of Life.

Michael: *I studied with JJ Hurtak for over forty years. Hurtak lives in Sedona, Arizona, but he usually travels teaching worldwide.*

Sai Baba East Indian Guru

"Selfless service alone gives the needed strength and courage to awaken the sleeping humanity in one's heart." ~ Sai Baba

The Sai Baba Organization undertakes service activities as a means to spiritual advancement. Sai Baba manifested Vibhuti (holy ash) and small objects.

Michael: *In December 1990, I stayed at the Sai Baba ashram for one month. One day, Sai Baba stopped in front of me, and I touched his feet. When I returned to Los Angeles, boils broke out in my body. I was being purified. Sai Baba has been with me all my life. In 1991, I started teaching hands-on healing in Laho Chi. Sai Baba overlighted the healing.*

Babaji Kriya Yoga

"Who vows to sacrifice all in the quest of the Divine is fit to unravel the final mysteries of life through the science of meditation." ~ Babaji

Michael: *I learned Kriya Yoga from an instructor in Sedona. It is eighteen Yoga postures of Hatha Yoga.*

Yogananda

"As a river has a source, so the river of consciousness has a source. It descends from Cosmic Consciousness. The consciousness of God is beyond all creation." ~ Yogananda

"Of greatest help in your development is the habit of mental whispering to God. You will see a change in yourself that you will like very much. No matter what you do, God should be constantly in your mind." ~ Yogananda

Michael: *I visited the Yogananda Center in Los Angeles while living in L.A.*

Brahma Baba Brahma Kumari's

25 – Service Consciousness: How to Live in the Present Moment

"I cannot offer more than what I am. Therefore, the greatest service I can give the world is self-transformation. When I am transformed, I can give a new me to the world." ~ Brahma Kumari's

Brahma Baba is the founder of Brahma Kumaris. He had a series of visions in 1936. The Brahma Kumari's are over one million, mostly women. Their presence is in more than one hundred and twenty countries.

The Brahma Kumari's are a spiritual group that teaches Raja Yoga. This yoga is without rituals or mantras. It is about silencing your mind. Anyone can access this meditation.

One center, Peace Village, welcomes thousands of people worldwide. It is located on a campus in the Catskill Mountains of New York.

The Brahma Kumaris are in service to the upliftment of humanity.

Michael: *I have two friends who regularly go to Peace Village for meditation retreats. They meditate, connecting with Brahma Baba. I also connect daily with Baba, who is one of my spiritual guides.*

This is Judy Roger's story of her journey and experience of Service Consciousness.

Judy Roger is a student and organizer of the Brahma Kumaris. She also is a teacher of Raj Yoga meditation for 27 years. Since 2006 she has lived in the Brahma Kumaris' Peace Village Retreat north of New York City.

Judy's interest in raja yoga meditation, as taught by the Brahma Kumaris, led to an extended study of consciousness and applied spirituality, focusing on how the quality of our awareness affects our thoughts, vision, and experience in the world. Over the past twenty-five years, she has returned to India roughly forty times to continue her study and practice of raj yoga and has supported many Brahma Kumaris initiatives. In 2009, she co-authored a book on altruism called *Something Beyond Greatness*.

She divides her time between her consultant and communication strategist work and her commitment to a raja yoga meditation practice.

Judy: *At some point in my late thirties, I felt an inner tug to think about deeper things, a spiritual curiosity. Also, I was working in media and living in Chicago, but life was empty. I found a book by Edgar Cayce and read it cover-to-cover. I liked it so much that I went in search of others. One of the things he talks about frequently is "the Akashic records." When peering into someone's life, he looked into their Akashic records. So, a year or so after I started reading these books, I saw a class on Akashic Record Reading and signed up.*

The class was held on a Saturday in a room at a hotel. When I walked in, there were about 35 people in the room, but I only knew one, my chiropractor. At the front of the room was a smiling, plump woman with thinning hair and a Texan accent. She started right out as soon as we all were seated, explaining that a shaman from Central America had taught her a prayer that opened the Akashic records. She printed the prayer on a slip of paper and handed it to all of us. We were to repeat the prayer three times, twice out loud and once silently inserting the full name of the person whose records we were reading. That was it. Then, she told us to partner with someone and read their Akashic records. I was

25 – Service Consciousness: How to Live in the Present Moment

pretty sure this wouldn't go well, but I partnered with a man who seemed to have a lot of confidence. I suggested that he "read" first. He did a pretty good job. He seemed to pick up some things about my life. Then we switched. I told him that I had never done such a thing before and not to expect much. So, I said the prayer three times, inserting his name, and as I looked at him, I saw two subtle faces over his head: a young girl and a young boy. "You have two children," I said. He nodded. "The girl is very unhappy with you." He nodded again. So, for the next few minutes, I seemed to be able to "see" some of the things going on in his life. After that, I did Akashic record readings for a few people. Then I stopped but was hooked on the need to know more about this hidden world of spirituality.

I began seeking in earnest, looking for truth. I wasn't searching for God but for the answers to the most significant questions: who are we really? What is the meaning of all the things that are happening around us? I went to lectures on spiritual topics and sought spiritual bookstores wherever I went.

I entered a spiritual group called The Movement of Spiritual Inner Awakening. *A curly-haired man led it from California. Its most famous member was Ariana Huffington. MSIA, as it was called, required studying books and receiving a mantra as part of an initiation. I spent about two years trying this path. About that time, I began taking Insight courses. These were a bit spiritual and more about personal development, kind of like EST. I went to a series of retreats, learning even more about myself. Though I liked MSIA, I was still seeking it. I found my way into a Sai Baba group. They were very nice people who met in a rented space. They all made food, brought it, and finished each meeting with a shared meal. They also did a lot of social service. I liked the Indian flavor* of the group and their service, but their practice seemed to be constant chanting. "Where was the silence?" I wondered. So, I stopped going.

Around that time, I was invited to a women's program in Boston. It wasn't explicitly spiritual, but it did have spiritual elements. When the day came, I had developed a bad cold. I went, but my head was so stuffy that I sat quietly through most of it, watching as if I was looking into a room from the outside. A few months later, the woman who had invited me asked me if I would be interested in meeting a spiritual leader from India. "Sure," I said. So, she gave me an address in the Western suburbs of Chicago. That was the day that changed everything.

I drove over an hour to get to the townhouse where the meeting was held. When I entered the room, there were about thirty people there. I only knew the one who had invited me. After a few minutes, our hostess invited us to come sit in a circle. Then, three women in white saris entered the room. One of them was very small and only spoke Hindi. Her name was Dadi Janki.

We started by going around the circle and introducing ourselves. When I introduced myself, she said (through a translator), "I feel like we have met before." I said that I was having the same feeling. After introducing ourselves, she said, "I'm going to talk about truth." I perked up — Finally! This is what I had been looking for. I no longer remember what she said that night. I know that everything in my being resonated with her and what she shared. She invited me to the Brahma Kumaris Center the next day at seven am. The center was just a five-minute drive from my home.

The following day, I arrived at the center at the stroke of seven am. I took my seat in the packed room. There was a starburst image at *the front of the room and a large black-and-white photo of a pleasant-looking older man on the wall. One of the women in a sari from the night before was in the front of the room. She explained that this morning was the "rakhi" festival, an Indian festival of purity. Each of us was to stay in our seats in yoga until it was our turn to come up. We were to sit on a stool in front of Dadi Janki when we came up.*

Then, we extended our right arm. She would tie a rakhi bracelet on our wrist, signifying a bond of God's love and protection. We would then come to the sister sitting next to her to get a blessing card and a sweet. It seemed straightforward enough. So, I sat in yoga until it was my turn. Then, I went up to the stool in front of Dadi Janki. I sat on the stool and looked into her eyes. She smiled sweetly at me and motioned for me to extend my arm. As she tied the rakhi bracelet, she never took her eyes off mine. I looked into her eyes and began to see and experience things inside. Above her head, I saw an outpouring of light, and I felt my heart pounding. I felt a flood of love – not the normal kind of love of family but a bigger waterfall of love. I was connected to something much bigger and more beautiful than I had ever known. I realized there was a whole unseen world where the truth about all of us was living. I resolved to do everything in my power to understand and embrace this truth.

That was almost thirty years ago. That day, I began studying and meditating with the Brahma Kumaris, first in Chicago and then in Boston. I finally moved into a retreat center, where I have been for almost twenty years.

Books for Further Study:

Overself Awakening by J.J. Hurtak, Keys of Enoch website.

72 Stages Conscious Awakening by J.J. Hurtak, Keys of Enoch website.

The Gene Keys by Richard Rudd.

The Power of Now by Eckhart Tolle.

May this self-help nonfiction book assist you. Start looking at your inner patterns of childhood wounding. Say "Yes" to notice and acknowledge pain in your body. Feel the discomfort and breathe into it. Your finances, health, and relationships may be affected.

About the Author

Michael David Lawrience

Michael David Lawrience is an author, energy healer, intuitive, and self-help mentor, known for his transformative works, including his books *The Secret for Freedom from Drama, Trauma and Pain* and *A Better Life Through Spiritual Growth and Higher Consciousness*.

With a background in business (B.Com) and (B.A.) Sacred Healing/Spirituality, and fifteen years of certification as a Bowen Therapist. Michael draws on over thirty years of study in spiritual teachings like JJ Hurtak's *Keys of Enoch*.

Through his writing and mentorship, he empowers readers to leverage their emotions, thoughts, and bodily awareness to navigate life's challenges. His blog features over 200 articles covering topics like codependency, emotional healing, and spiritual awakening, all aimed at fostering personal growth. www.emotionalhealthtips.com.

Michael and his wife, Lyn, reside in the stunning Red Rocks of Sedona, Arizona. He enjoys nature and hiking the local vortex trails.

Michael offers a free Kindle copy of his latest book, *A Better Life Through Spiritual Growth and Higher Consciousness*, inviting readers to experience its insights and transformative tools. If you'd like a copy, send him your e-mail address, and he'll send it to you as a gift. He'd appreciate a review. For your copy, you can visit his website or reach out to him directly at:

www.emotionalhealthtips.com/books-michael-lawrience

www.ingramcontent.com/pod-product-compliance
Lightning Source LLC
LaVergne TN
LVHW021235080526
838199LV00088B/4358